Sam Sorbo offers brilliant, inspired, and thoughtful devotional reflections in *Teach from Love* for any family or school group interested in drawing closer to God. I commend Sam and her ability to open up the truth of Jesus Christ and His Word written.

—TED BAEHR, *founder and publisher of* Movieguide®,
*chairman of the Christian Film & Television Commission,
educator, and media pundit*

We removed the Bible from public schools but failed to consider how children would come to learn godly characteristics. In this devotional, Sam Sorbo uses parables and Bible stories to introduce strong values for discussion within families and classrooms. Parents, teachers, and school administrators—this is for you!

—EVERETT PIPER, *president,
Oklahoma Wesleyan University; author,* Not a Daycare

Teach from Love is a great devotion for any family seeking to raise godly adults. The verses and questions to discuss with your family during the school year will greatly benefit you and your children's souls.

—ROBERT BORTINS, CEO, *Classical Conversations;
chairman,* Homeschool Now USA

We have allowed the ungodly to rule! We have allowed them to influence our culture, dictate our norms, and educate our children. We have seen the results and are pushing back the darkness. Sam Sorbo has given us an excellent tool in that pushback. Teaching the way Jesus taught, using parables and stories, Sam allows you to absorb the issues a̶n̶d̶ ̶ ̶ ̶ ̶ ̶ ̶ ̶ ̶ ̶ ̶ ̶ ̶ ̶ ̶ ̶ ̶ ̶ spirit. She provides great insigh̶ ̶ ̶ ̶ ̶

—MASON V̶

D0451658

Teach from Love is for families everywhere. Sam Sorbo has scratched where most families itch, having created a family devotional that begins and ends with the school year. The chapters are focused, each daily lesson is fully supplied, and every page is designed to instill godly character in the hearts of your children. As a dad who has longed for a resource like this, the search is over with *Teach from Love*.

—TODD WILSON, *founder, Familyman Ministries*

Teach from Love empowers today's Christian family to grow daily in the grace and knowledge of God. Sam Sorbo delivers a powerful, practical tool that's perfect for kids, families, and classrooms everywhere.

—BILL BLANKSCHAEN, *author, co-author of*
You Will Be Made to Care, *homeschooling father of six,*
and former Christian school principal

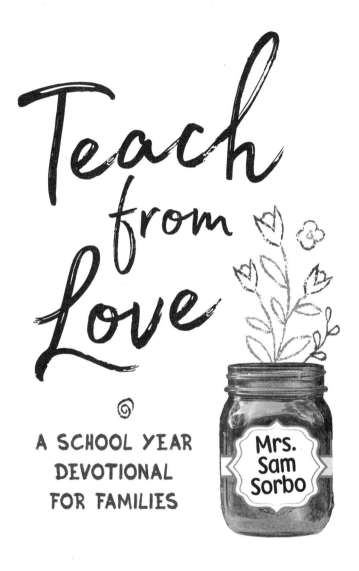

Teach from Love

from

Love

A SCHOOL YEAR DEVOTIONAL FOR FAMILIES

Mrs. Sam Sorbo

BroadStreet
PUBLISHING

BroadStreet Publishing ® Group, LLC
Racine, Wisconsin, USA
BroadStreetPublishing.com

Teach from Love: A SCHOOL YEAR DEVOTIONAL FOR FAMILIES

Stock or custom editions of BroadStreet Publishing titles may be purchased
in bulk for educational, business, ministry, fundraising, or sales promotional
use. For information, please e-mail info@broadstreetpublishing.com.

Cover design by Chris Garborg at garborgdesign.com
Typesetting by Katherine Lloyd at theDESKonline.com

Printed in the United States of America

17 18 19 20 21 5 4 3 2 1

This book is dedicated to my loving husband, Kevin, and our three incredible children, Braeden, Shane, and Octavia.

Contents

Foreword

I loved school. I was a complete jock, playing football, basketball, and baseball, and also getting in a few rounds of golf when I had the chance. My father was the junior high science teacher, and I had three older siblings go through the system before me, so I was involved even before I got there. I boasted perfect attendance, I drove a powder-blue Mustang that I bought with my paper route money, and I still maintain several of my high school friendships today. To call my high school years the halcyon days of scholarship, sports, and social life might even be an understatement.

My wife, Sam, loved learning but hated the institution. With an exceptional mind, she was bored and reportedly socially awkward, and school became for her a source of anxiety and discomfort. She often stayed home, claiming illness; however, because her grades were excellent, she was never reprimanded.

Our little boy not only took after me with his social skills but also surpassed my highest expectations. He made friends with everyone; in the grocery store, he would strike up a conversation with someone in the vegetable aisle from his seat in the cart. It was with excitement that we sent our oldest child to the local public school. By the middle of second grade, though, we realized that things were not quite what we'd hoped for. The ethics and values Sam and I had learned in school had faded or disappeared, and the academics were less rigorous than we expected. Because we travel a great deal as well, we decided to try home education.

That decision led us on a journey of discovery that continues to inspire and astound us. On this journey, we have come to understand the incredible gifts of moral principles and faith that are frequently overlooked in our schools today. Our shared Christian heritage is something to be treasured, not ignored. Indeed, it is something that requires continual vigilance and nurturing.

Our schools define their goals as "college prep and career readiness," but is that all we desire for our offspring? There is much more to life than a job, and more to education than a mere career or continued schooling.

This devotional intends to help guide the school family to focus on what God wishes for each of His children, so our kids may discover His purpose in their lives.

Conversation leads to relationship, and relationship is what life is all about. That is the most important thing we can teach our children, so they may find a closer relationship with their Creator in heaven.

Kevin Sorbo

Welcome

Little children, let us not love in word or talk
but in deed and in truth.

JOHN 3:18 ESV

*D*ressed in a floral shirt and jeans and carrying a giggling toddler on her hip, a harried woman approached the table where I was about to sign copies of my book, *They're YOUR Kids: An Inspirational Journey from Self-Doubter to Home School Advocate*. She asked me, "Do you think the schools really aren't capable of instilling good morals in our children?"

My talk at this church event, explaining the enormous benefits of home education, had run late, and I was just sitting down to sign books. Although my signing line was growing, the woman before me was clearly distraught, compelling me to address her concerns. My brief presentation had not entirely convinced her, so I approached it from a different angle.

"If I enroll my child in art classes, will he learn calculus?"

She looked at me, confused, then shook her head. "No."

"It's really that simple. We do not ask the schools to teach anything related to God. On the contrary, schools often teach notions that are antithetical to belief in God, so how will godly values enter the classroom?"

"I don't know. I guess just by the Golden Rule or something, right? I mean, kids learn kindness and sharing and respect for the teacher and stuff in school."

"True. That's mainly true. And it's true that in art class, my son will learn some math—proportions or geometry, perhaps, but not linear algebra or differential equations. It really just depends on how in-depth you want your children to be with God."

"Well, maybe they should just get that education at home," she challenged.

No argument from me on that point. "Of course, you're right. Education—all education—starts at home."

Satisfied, she smiled, placed her book on the table in front of me, and asked me to sign it, *To Amber, It's WORTH it! Sam Sorbo*.

After that encounter, it dawned on me that there ought to be a training handbook for teaching biblical values to our children on a daily basis. Obviously, the Bible is the best resource on that topic, but sometimes, for busy families, it's shrewder to have something broken down and organized into little nuggets to chew on each day. All families, whether they home school or enroll their children at some scholastic institution, can and should shepherd their children in morally grounded values and ethics. Private Christian schools and teachers, in general, would similarly benefit from this kind of approach.

I reflected on my class of seventh graders (I shepherd a Challenge A class through Classical Conversations, a national home school program, one day each week). I write a word on the board that expresses a moral characteristic, and we begin our weekly full-day seminar with a short devotional. First, I ask the class for definitions of the word, and then antonyms. These I also write on the board, then I take all suggestions from the students, encouraging them to simply blurt out their ideas. I call this *workshopping* the concept. Once we have a comprehensive understanding of the moral quality, we examine what it looks like in practice, and also how life appears when this characteristic is absent.

Through workshopping the word *patience*, I discovered that *anger* is its opposite. Think about that for a moment. What a revelation my students presented me!

The value in this study seems indisputable, but organizing it was my next hurdle. I intended this book to correspond with the school year. Therefore, there are thirty-six chapters for that many weeks. I have chosen seventy-two character qualities that any Christian should strive to exhibit, organizing them into groups of two for each week.

Why two? God gave us two eyes for binocular vision and two ears for surround sound, affording us enhanced perception of His three-dimensional world. Using two words encourages intense comparison and more profound discussion.

Challenge your children to contribute to the exploration of these terms and why God honors them. Select a time when you can regularly find fifteen minutes to pursue this devotional: early morning, peaceful evening, or quiet bedtime.

In this devotional, each week begins by introducing the two words, including a short assessment of how they relate to each other. I encourage you to take a little extra time discussing each of the characteristics, comparing and exploring them and their context with your children, setting up the Monday story. You could do this on Sunday on the way home from church or at lunch, or you could just use it Monday to launch your study. On the final page of each week, there is space for note-taking. Recording some of the observations during your initial discussion may prove interesting to review at the end of the week, but you can also use it throughout the week's study.

Each weekday begins with a Bible verse that relates to the words of the week. Then follows a story or commentary that demonstrates one of the words, or both in concert. Read all this to your family, followed by the short prayer. Encourage older children to contribute by having them read aloud. Take turns. Use the questions/prompts at the bottom of each page for discussion with your children. Offer your own answers to bolster their confidence in sharing. They will likely bless you with their insights and sagacity.

Later in the week there will be a short Bible story illustrating the topics of the week. We know that God has provided a blueprint for human morality through fascinating characters and their stories in the Bible, and we can all learn from their behavior and their relationships with the one true God.

The Friday page summarizes the work you've done during the week to explore and embrace the qualities God desires in all His children. Those may be the most thought-provoking and insightful questions.

Last comes the final "Annotations" page where you've jotted down the clever or surprising things your children have shared with you, as well as any of your own discoveries. It is those moments I encourage you to savor, so be sure to avail yourself of this space to record anything during the week that seems significant—and even some stuff that doesn't. This study should be fun. You could also use the blank space to note goals or ideas you seek to implement as a family. At the end of the year, won't it be fascinating to see how you and your children have grown in the Lord?

There are two breaks—three weeks mirroring the Christmas and New Year holiday, and one week in conjunction with the Easter/spring recess.

My prayer for your family, as you embark on this journey exploring godly characteristics, is for you to grow your relationships with one another and our Creator. If we want a closer connection to God, and to act more Christian in everyday life, it isn't enough to simply desire it. We need training—a plan to follow.

As you seek to emulate Christ, allow this little book to serve as a roadmap for your entire family or class, to pursue Him in a more focused and intentional manner.

Sam Sorbo

Boldness and Fearlessness

Week
1

Stand Strong

For God has not given us a spirit of fear,
but of power and of love and of a sound mind.

2 TIMOTHY 1:7 NKJV

Corrie ten Boom was a Dutch watchmaker who helped Jews escape the Nazi Holocaust during World War II. Corrie's family was Christian, and as such, they believed the Jews to be God's chosen people. When their Jewish neighbors were forced to go into hiding like many other Jewish families, the ten Boom family sheltered them. The fearlessness of Corrie's family came from the knowledge that they were doing what was right in God's eyes.

Food was scarce and only available with a ration card at that time. Corrie shared with her family that she knew a man who worked at the rations office. She went to his house one night to ask for her family's cards. When he asked how many she needed, she surprised herself with her boldness, answering, "One hundred!" He gave them to her, and she supplied every Jew she could with a card.

Corrie didn't show a spirit of fear; instead, God gave her boldness and the power to save many lives. This week, allow God to fill you with boldness and fearlessness to accomplish His purposes.

Lord, give me courage and fill me with the power to do great things for you. Make me bold as I serve you.

- In what situations do you experience fear?
- How could boldness make you a more effective Christ follower?

No Limits

Whoever watches the wind will not plant;
whoever looks at the clouds will not reap.

ECCLESIASTES 11:4

*P*anphobia is the fear of everything. Individuals who have this disorder can experience feelings of anxiety and panic as a result of every passing thing. They often go years without leaving their homes due to fear of the unknown in the world around them. This impedes their ability to have normal relationships or hold jobs; their overcautiousness limits what they are able or willing to do. Imagine if the ten Boom family had been too afraid to hide Jews in their home. What if the Wright brothers hadn't been bold enough to attempt to build a flying machine?

In Ecclesiastes 11, King Solomon warns that being too consumed with watching the wind prevents people from planting their fields (for fear the wind will blow the seeds away). He also observes that if farmers are overly concerned with the clouds in the sky and worried about whether it will rain, they will never reap what they've sown. Fear is the ultimate straightjacket, but when we allow God to fill us with His power, love, and boldness, there are no limits to our abilities.

Lord, help me to recognize fear and acknowledge it as satan's way to put boundaries on God's people.

- Who do you think has lived a fearless life and why?
- When was a time that fear kept you from doing something God called you to do?

Five Stones

Now, Lord, consider their threats and enable your servants
to speak your word with great boldness.

Acts 4:29

*D*avid was the stereotypical little brother, wanting to hang out with his big brothers, but he was too small and had other obligations. While his older siblings were off fighting for King Saul, David tended his father's sheep.

One day, the armies of King Saul were in the Valley of Elah and facing the Philistine army. One of the Philistines was a giant—literally. According to the account in 1 Samuel 17, he stood nine feet six inches. Every day this giant, Goliath, swaggered into the valley between the two sides and shouted taunts at the Israelite army and mocked their God.

David's father, Jesse, sent him to bring food to his brothers in their camp, and David heard the insults Goliath yelled. Filled with anger over Goliath's disrespect of the Almighty, David volunteered to fight the enemy. The shepherd boy was just a lad, so King Saul had doubts, but no other fighters were brave enough to offer. When David declared the Lord would help him do it, Saul conceded.

David gathered five smooth stones and did what he said he would do—he slayed the giant. His boldness came from God. When you are in God's will and are fighting for Him, there is no reason for fear. God will grant courage and provide the stones.

Heavenly Father, give me the boldness of David when it comes to living for you.

- What are the "giants" in your life?
- What "stones" has God given you to slay them?

Bragging Rights

"But let the one who boasts boast about this: that they have the understanding to know me, that I am the Lord, who exercises kindness, justice and righteousness on earth, for in these I delight," declares the LORD.

JEREMIAH 9:24

*H*ave you ever met someone who was overconfident? Someone who couldn't stop talking about how great she was and how much she had accomplished? Confidence is a great quality to have, but too much can turn people away. No one wants to be around a know-it-all or a braggart. This week's character traits, boldness and fearlessness, are admirable, but without the right motivation or heart behind them, they can be destructive.

The ten Boom family showed boldness. Their courage derived from service to God, not self. David's fearlessness in the face of a giant came from his confidence that the Lord would help him and his desire to quiet the blaspheming Philistine.

Arrogance, or overconfidence, is often rooted in self: "I want you to know how great *I* am." Instead, we should focus on how great *God* is. As the prophet Jeremiah said in today's passage, if you are going to boast, boast about the Lord. He is the one who deserves all the glory.

Father, help me keep my boldness and fearlessness rooted in you. Thank you for being such a great God.

- When was a time you experienced someone who was overconfident? How did that impact you?
- How can you balance being bold with being overconfident? How does God fit into that process?

Just a Little Extra

In the same way, faith by itself,
if it is not accompanied by action, is dead.

JAMES 2:17

*E*xtraordinary is just ordinary with something "extra" added. Both Corrie ten Boom and young David had something in common: they started as ordinary people who were willing to take action for the Lord. The power of Almighty God was the "extra" in their lives. With God, anything is possible.

It's one thing to believe that, but a whole new level of faith is required to put action behind that belief. Combining belief with action allows boldness and fearlessness to shine.

These two invaluable qualities are behind some of the greatest missionaries ever known—the apostle Paul, Lottie Moon, Eric Liddell, Jim Elliot, and George Muller, to name a few. In their own power, they could not have spread the gospel in the amazing ways they did. Through the power of God, these everyday Christ followers became extraordinary soul winners for the kingdom of Christ, and honorable examples for the rest of us.

God wants all of us to combine our faith with action. Will you give God your ordinary and allow him to give you the something "extra"?

God, motivate me to put action behind my faith, and give me boldness and fearlessness in my walk with you.

- Where is God calling you to add action to your faith?
- When you stepped forward boldly in faith, what happened next?

Annotations

Combining your faith with action often necessitates both boldness and fearlessness. When God is the root of your confidence and courage, nothing is impossible.

....
....
....
....
....
....
....
....
....
....
....
....
....
....
....
....
....
....
....
....
....
....
....
....
....
....
....
....

Virtue and Moral Excellence

Week
2

Checking the Weather

Do not conform to the pattern of this world,
but be transformed by the renewing of your mind.

ROMANS 12:2

*R*ight after six-year-old Kenny got back from the store with his new white tennis shoes, the rain began to fall. Although he had fun with his friends, jumping through the puddles and splashing around, the mud ruined his shoes, leaving a lasting stain. Kenny learned the hard way to stay on the sidewalk when it rained.

In the same way, following the crowd may not only leave you with muddy shoes but could also result in a tarnished reputation. The Bible says not to "conform to the pattern of this world." Instead, we are to conform to moral excellence and virtue, embracing a high standard of what is right in the eyes of God—staying out of the mud, spiritually.

A mucky mess happens when water hits dirt. You may not be walking through puddles, but a higher standard may be to avoid the rain altogether. The Bible tells us not to murder, but Jesus goes further, telling us not to even think angry thoughts about our brother. Jesus modeled that virtuous higher standard for us. As Kenny learned, walking through puddles in white sneakers isn't a good idea—and neither is following the crowd when they lead you into areas that could tarnish your reputation.

Lord, help me protect my virtue and live with moral excellence.

- When have you "walked in mud" when you should've "stayed on the sidewalk"?
- What does a virtuous person of high moral standards look like to you?

Be Different

So I say, walk by the Spirit,
and you will not gratify the desires of the flesh.

GALATIANS 5:16

Turn on prime-time television and you're likely to find numerous examples of sin and indulgence. They are the exact opposite of this week's characteristics—virtue and moral excellence. The root of sin is *self*, and indulgence means giving in to one's self. The common denominator? You guessed it—self. "Be true to yourself." "Follow your heart." "Take time for you." These are just a few of the misguided philosophies prevalent today.

While none of these are inherently wrong, they do distract us from where we should focus—on Christ. Jesus said, "Whoever wants to be my disciple must deny themselves and take up their cross and follow me" (Matthew 16:24). Living a life of moral excellence means dying to our wants and desires, and choosing to put God first.

That's not an easy or popular choice. Sometimes it involves choosing clothing, music, and movies that honor God, when we really want to wear, listen to, or watch something else. In this crazy me-first world, choose to be different.

Lord, show me areas where I need to deny self, and give me a desire for moral excellence.

- Would others be pointed to Christ through your clothing, television, and music selection? Why or why not?
- In what areas do you struggle to deny self and strive to be different?

Wednesday

Wise Choice

Now for this very reason also, applying all diligence,
in your faith supply moral excellence,
and in your moral excellence, knowledge.

2 PETER 1:5 NASB

*J*immy left the grocery store and noticed a wallet lying on the ground. It had money in it and an ID. He'd spent more on groceries than expected and that money would help make ends meet. He could pocket the money without anyone knowing, but having moral excellence, he chose to return it all to the store. He knew the money wasn't his to take.

Sometimes doing the right thing doesn't pay, but it does make you feel good. The Holy Spirit grants a feeling of peace over the situation. Circumstances arise daily, both at home and at school, when you must make a choice about whether you will have integrity or indulge in self. Living a virtuous life means not choosing to take a shortcut when running a race, letting a clerk know if they haven't charged you enough, cleaning up messes you are responsible for creating, and owning up to the mistakes you've made. Having integrity is choosing the right thing even when no one is watching.

Sometimes that choice is the hardest to make properly. Many voices in society today urge us to serve ourselves instead of our heavenly Father. Jimmy made the strong choice to do what was right in God's eyes, to honor Him before self. Choose moral excellence; your reward is eternal.

Father, please help me honor you in all my decisions through the power of the Holy Spirit.

- When was a time when you had to choose integrity or self?
- How does having moral excellence create an eternal reward?

With Honor

Do you not know that your bodies are temples
of the Holy Spirit, who is in you, whom you have received
from God? You are not your own; you were bought
at a price. Therefore honor God with your bodies.

1 CORINTHIANS 6:19–20

Imagine a world without leaders—no teachers, no police officers, no governors, no Congress, no president. That's what would happen if we lived in a world without virtue and moral integrity. President Dwight Eisenhower reportedly said that the supreme quality for leadership was undoubtedly integrity. He held that without it, no real success was possible, not on a football field, in an army, or even in office.

Moral excellence and virtue lead to trust. When Jesus and His disciples came to Capernaum, the tax collectors asked Peter if Jesus paid temple taxes. Peter unwittingly answer yes. Knowing this, when Jesus saw Peter, he pointed out that kings of the earth don't collect taxes from their own children. In other words, as the Son of God, Jesus viewed the temple tax as unnecessary. Even so, having integrity, Jesus sent Peter to catch a fish with enough money inside it to pay both their taxes. Christ recognized that choosing virtue and offering payment even when He didn't rightfully owe it would set a good example and draw others to His leadership.

God, help me to live with integrity and walk as a godly leader.

- What can you do to show leadership qualities in different areas of your life?
- How can Christian leaders make a difference in the world?

Friday

Whatever

Finally, brethren, whatever things are true, whatever things
are noble, whatever things are just, whatever things are
pure, whatever things are lovely, whatever things are
of good report, if there is any virtue and if there
is anything praiseworthy—meditate on these things.

PHILIPPIANS 4:8 NKJV

True, noble, just, pure, lovely, good report, virtuous, and praiseworthy—that's quite a list of characteristics! Today's Scripture
passage tells us to meditate on whatever reflects those descriptors.
Meditate means to focus your thoughts for an extended period.
Like a bag of tea, good thoughts need to steep a while to help create a rich flavor. By choosing to think about the positive, you are
controlling your behavior by first controlling your thoughts. This
is the first step to living a life with virtue and moral excellence.

Think back on the areas we've covered this week—not blindly
following the crowd, confidently denying self, showing unflinch-
ing integrity, and exhibiting responsible leadership skills. Consider
how these characteristics appear in your own life, or how to
encourage their development. Understand that focusing on the
positive and striving to live with virtue and moral excellence, in
whatever way that may take shape, brings you closer to God.

**Lord, guard my thoughts and let me meditate on things that
will praise and honor you.**

- What is one change you can make today to show higher
  virtue and solid moral excellence?
- How can choosing to live by these standards affect your
  future?

Annotations

Living a life of virtue and moral excellence means taking the narrow path of righteousness when everyone else seems to be traveling the easy or more fun route.

Attentiveness and Dedication

Week
3

Hey There!

We must pay the most careful attention, therefore,
to what we have heard, so that we do not drift away.

HEBREWS 2:1

"*M*iriam, would you read the next part of our story?" Mom looked over to see Miriam staring at a bird on the window sill. "Miriam?"

"Oh, sorry, Mom. I was just looking out the window."

"Sweetheart, please pay attention to what we are doing. When you are attentive, you show me that what I am saying to you is important."

One of the best ways to show respect for others is to give them undivided attention especially during a conversation. Focusing on the needs of others helps you get to know them deeper. Engagement is the root of relationship, and paying attention is the start of engagement.

Of course, allowing herself to be distracted by what was outside the window was not only wasteful of Mom's time, but Miriam also forfeited her involvement in the work before her. It's never enough to simply appear to be paying attention. Giving a person your undivided attention—even from electronic distractions—means fully concentrating on that person without thinking about anything else.

In your next conversation, look the other person in the eye and focus your thinking only on what he is saying.

Lord, let me show my love to all those I encounter by giving them my full attention.

- How does it feel when someone does not give her full attention to you?
- What is one way to show others you are paying careful attention to what they are saying?

Dangerous Neglect

For lack of discipline they will die,
led astray by their own great folly.

F olly. That word is seldom used these days, but it represents neglecting what is smart and instead doing something foolish or reckless.

For example, Brian rode his bike to school every day. He loved the fresh air and meeting up with his friends on the way. One day he saw his friend Nathan coming down the road to meet him. Brian was almost at the corner as he waved to his buddy. In fact, he was so excited to see Nathan that he failed to look to his left. He didn't see Mrs. Goucher pushing her baby stroller.

Brian arrived at the corner at about the same time as Mrs. Goucher, and his front tire nicked the front tire of the stroller.

"Brian!" she yelled. "Pay attention to where you're going!"

He stomped on his brakes, catching himself before falling. "I am so sorry. Are you okay?"

"We're fine," she said, "but you need to look both ways when you approach a corner."

Brian learned a valuable lesson that day: neglecting to follow the rules can have serious consequences. The same is true of us spiritually. Being attentive to God's commands will keep us from making foolish mistakes.

Lord, help me to always pay attention to your directions.

- When have you lost focus and suffered the consequences?
- What can we do to concentrate our attention on others in a way that encourages them?

Decisions, Decisions

Trust in the Lord with all your heart and lean not on your
own understanding; in all your ways submit to him,
and he will make your paths straight.

<small>PROVERBS 3:5–6</small>

*A*ccording to the Roberts Wesleyan College website and
other sites, adults make an average of 35,000 decisions each
day while children make 3,000.* Some of those decisions have to
do with our level of dedication to doing the right thing as a family
member, as a friend, as a student, or perhaps in a sports situation.

Andrew had to make a hard decision when his coach sched-
uled ball games during his church service time. Andrew loved
playing ball but decided that his commitment to God was more
important. Although he felt as if he was sacrificing his game time,
the benefits he gained from devoting that special time to his relationship with God paid even greater dividends in the long run.

Often the decisions we make involve processing information
that may seem confusing. Many answers may come to mind, but
God sees the big picture. He knows what is best for us, so we
need to get His input in all situations. He will guide us—if we'll
let Him.

Be attentive and dedicated in following God's directions. He
will not steer you wrong.

Lord, help me be attentive to your voice.

- Why is it important to list both pros and cons when you
  are trying to make a decision?
- Why was Andrew's sacrifice not really a sacrifice at all?

---

* Joel Hoomans, "35,000 Decisions: The Great Choices of Strategic Leaders,"
Roberts Wesleyan College, March 20, 2015, http://go.roberts.edu/leadingedge/
the-great-choices-of-strategic-leaders.

Listen to God's Voice

The Lord came and stood there, calling as at
the other times, "Samuel! Samuel!" Then Samuel said,
"Speak, for your servant is listening."

1 SAMUEL 3:10

As a boy, Samuel ministered under the priest, Eli, so he spent his days and nights in the temple. One night in the darkness, Samuel heard someone call his name. He thought it was Eli and went to the priest and answered him.

"I did not call you," Eli said.

This happened again. Then when Samuel came to Eli a third time, Eli realized the Lord was calling Samuel. He instructed him to go back to bed, and told him that if he heard the call again to acknowledge that it was God's voice.

The next time Samuel heard his name called, he replied, "Speak, for your servant is listening." He was attentive to God's call.

From that point on, Samuel always listened to God's voice. He knew God was with him and that God would give him the instruction he needed.

Our eternal God didn't speak only during biblical times. He speaks to people today, although it's often not out loud. Many times, we "hear" it only in our hearts. God also speaks to us through His Word and the words of other people.

Lord, make me always sensitive to hearing your voice in whatever way you choose to speak.

- Describe a time when God has spoken to you.
- When God speaks to your heart, how can you know it is Him?

Attentiveness and Dedication Are Important

Do not conform to the pattern of this world,
but be transformed by the renewing of your mind.
Then you will be able to test and approve what
God's will is—his good, pleasing and perfect will.

ROMANS 12:2

*A*ttentiveness and dedication are important godly characteristics that intersect. If we are dedicated to being the best we can be in God's kingdom, we must be attentive to God's voice as He shows us His way for our lives.

This week we have seen how important it is to listen. Being attentive applies to schoolwork, to friends, to all relationships. It means going beyond "How are you doing?" and "I'm good" to really delve into the events in another person's life. It is the difference between doing something correctly the first time, like a school or work assignment, or needing to go back and start it over. Not paying attention at the right time can result in severe consequences, like when Brian nearly rode his bike into the baby stroller.

Practicing attentiveness opens the mind to hearing when God is communicating too. He has a plan for your life, but if you don't pay attention to His guidance, in whatever form it may come, and dedicate yourself to following His leading, the plan will not come to fruition. Always listen for what God says. He is attentive to you, so pay Him the same respect back.

Lord, it is not always easy to know the right thing to do. Give me wisdom and discernment to hear your voice.

- What is one key to being a good listener?
- How might we better exemplify attentiveness and dedication to others?

Annotations

God gave us ears, but we also need to listen with our hearts. Always be ready to hear God's voice. Dedicate yourself to being attentive to God and to others.

....

....

....

....

....

....

....

....

....

....

....

....

....

....

....

....

....

....

....

....

....

....

....

....

....

Obedience and Devotion

Week
4

Rooted

So that you would walk in a manner worthy of the God
who calls you into His own kingdom and glory.

1 Thessalonians 2:12 nasb

The root is an important part of a plant. It procures minerals and water from the soil and anchors the plant so external elements won't knock it down. Roots also store food for the future.

Jesus once told a parable about a farmer sowing seeds. Some of the seeds were sown on rocky ground where there wasn't enough soil. The seed sprouted quickly but then withered away when the sun came, because it didn't have enough roots. True roots run deep, and Christians with deep roots show obedience and devotion.

The root of the word *devotion* is *devote*, from the Latin word *devotus*, the past participle of *devoveo*, which means "to vow." A vow shows steadfast commitment, which implies and dictates obedience. As you begin this week, consider your root in Christ and think of how He feeds you, saying, "I am the bread of life" (John 6:48). He also gives you "hope as an anchor for [your] soul" (Hebrews 6:19), and provides for your future: "But seek first his kingdom ... and all these things will be given to you" (Matthew 6:33).

Lord, as I meditate on your Word, may I reaffirm my obedience and devotion to you.

- What are some specific ways you can show devotion to someone you love?
- How can you demonstrate complete obedience to God?

Deliberate Devotion

If anyone, then, knows the good they ought
to do and doesn't do it, it is sin for them.

JAMES 4:17

*G*race hummed as she sat in the back seat on the way to school.

"Please stop humming," her older brother called from the front.

"I can hum if I want to," she told him defiantly, and her humming then got louder. She bopped her head back and forth as if to prove her right to hum.

Finally, her mom said, "Okay, Grace. That's enough humming."

Grace's mouth was silent, but her lips still pursed in a pretend hum and her head still bopped back and forth. She looked at the back of her brother's head with squinted eyes.

Her mom tried not to chuckle because she knew Grace was humming defiantly on the inside.

Every parent dreams of obedient children, but obedience isn't just following orders. It's doing it with a happy heart. The opposite of that is willfulness: knowing what to do but choosing to do the opposite. When we understand God's Word but ignore His commands, we are being willfully disobedient. It's like standing face-to-face with God and shouting, "No!" Perhaps we're following Him, but like Grace, we're humming on the inside.

Father, forgive me when I am willfully disobedient.

- In what areas of your life are you humming on the inside?
- How do you respond when God tells you to do something you don't want to do?

Get Moving

He replied, "Blessed rather are those
who hear the word of God and obey it."

LUKE 11:28

*W*alking out the door to the grocery store, Carol remembered she hadn't turned on the dishwasher. The cycle took two hours, and if she waited until she returned, there would be no clean plates for her dinner party later that night. "Faith, please turn on the dishwasher for me," she told her teenage daughter. "Don't forget!" However, when she returned, Faith was in the same spot in front of the TV as when she left, and the dishwasher hadn't been started.

Jesus gave a command right before He left too: "Therefore go and make disciples of all nations, baptizing them in the name of the Father and of the Son and of the Holy Spirit, and teaching them to obey everything I have commanded you" (Matthew 28:19–20). He asked us to share the good news of the gospel with everyone and teach them to obey Him as well.

If we are truly devoted and obedient, we will start with our neighbors and move into our community and beyond to share the good news of Christ. Don't let Jesus find you in the same spot when He returns!

God, move me to obedience in the Great Commission, and open my eyes to discover those who need to know you.

- What friends of yours need to hear the good news of Christ?
- How does sharing the gospel show true devotion to God?

What If?

Through him we received grace and apostleship
to call all the Gentiles to the obedience that
comes from faith for his name's sake.

ROMANS 1:5

If you went to the ice cream parlor and found they were giving away free ice cream all month, you would tell all your friends. You would want them to share in the goodness. Now, do you feel the same about telling others about the free gift of eternal life through Christ? What if no one knew? What if the disciples never told anyone after Jesus died and rose again? What if the gospel truth was never shared throughout the world?

What if the Bible was never written? What if you had no way to read God's Word? What if there were no churches or bodies of believers to worship and learn together each week?

You are reading this devotion today because someone was obedient. Obedient to tell others that Jesus is alive, obedient to write down the words inspired by God, obedient to take the gospel to other nations, and obedient to share all that with you. Thank the Lord for the obedience of the many Christ followers who came before you.

Jesus, thank you for those who listened and obeyed your words. Let me be a fully devoted follower as well.

- Whose obedience to God has made it possible for you to hear the good news?
- How can you keep that good news going through your own obedience and devotion?

A Time to Sow

We demolish arguments and every pretension that sets
itself up against the knowledge of God, and we take
captive every thought to make it obedient to Christ.

2 CORINTHIANS 10:5

All plants must start from seed. On Monday we talked about the importance of the root to gather nutrients, anchor the plant, and provide food for the future. Before all that can happen, though, a seed must be selected. Any farmer will tell you the outcome of what you plant depends on the quality of the seed. Good seed will make a difference in the yield of a crop, in its appearance and vigor. Farmers also want seed that is pure—in other words, with a good lineage. They desire seeds that come from an untainted source.

Thoughts are like those seeds. A simple thought comes before any act of obedience, but which ones do you sow? Are your thoughts from a pure source with high quality? Today's verse says to demolish any thoughts that go against what you know to be true in God's Word. Before you can grow in Christ as a fully devoted follower, you must first carefully select which seeds you will sow.

Lord, help me to take captive my thoughts and to grow seeds of truth. Help me to bloom for you.

- What can you do to make sure you're planting the right seeds?
- How can planting the right seeds of thought help in your obedience and devotion to Christ?

Annotations

Obedience and devotion start within; they're a matter of the heart. When you plant seeds of truth, you will grow to obey God's Word and be fully devoted to Him.

Loyalty and Faithfulness

Week
5

A Loyal Friend

Jesus replied: "'Love the Lord your God with all your heart,
and with all your soul and with all your mind.'"

MATTHEW 22:37

*B*ob had been born with a serious birth defect. Because of
that, he couldn't participate in neighborhood softball games
and the other kids often made fun of him. Bob tried to act like it
was no big deal, but it hurt his feelings and he was lonely.

Bob was only eight when his family moved into a new neighborhood. Bob struggled to make friends in his new environment,
but luckily one nice boy, Jim, lived only a few houses away.

Jim was sad when he realized Bob couldn't play ball, and when
he saw a bully making fun of the new kid on the block, he was
mad. Jim decided that from that day on, Bob was going to have
a loyal friend.

Their friendship began when they were young boys, and it
persevered through adulthood. Jim was a faithful friend, determined to find games they could play together. He and Bob built
things and did science experiments.

Loyalty is the decision to be faithful, whether it's faithfulness
to God, our family and friends, our jobs, or our country. Faithfulness is the achievement of that goal. When we love God with
all our heart, soul, and mind, it instills a desire to be loyal and
faithful to Him and to others. Loving someone means showing
them loyalty.

Lord, help me to be loyal and faithful in all that I do.

- What are some practical ways to be loyal and faithful?
- How will it impact others if we have those traits?

A Blessing in Disguise

"Well done, good and faithful servant!
You have been faithful with a few things;
I will put you in charge of many things."

MATTHEW 25:21

*J*im's loyalty made a big difference in Bob's life. They both benefitted from their strong bonds of friendship, and learned things together, making lasting memories and cementing their relationship.

Loyalty is a choice. If Jim had opted to play ball with all the other neighborhood kids instead of hanging out with Bob, many negative things might have happened. Bob would certainly have been lonelier. Bullies could have destroyed his self-esteem. Bitterness and anger might have crept into his heart, impacting him for the rest of his life. If Jim had closed off his heart to being a loyal and faithful friend, he may never have cultivated the friendship that blessed him so mightily.

Because Jim responded with kindness and compassion, two lives were changed for the better. When we make the right choices, that brings joy to our souls—and it pleases God. It also provides a great example for others.

God honors loyalty and faithfulness. When God perceives those characteristics in a believer, He opens doors to bigger and better things.

God, help me to make wise choices.

- How can being faithful affect others?
- How can being faithful affect us?

Wednesday

Forever Friends

"Greater love has no one than this:
to lay down one's life for one's friends."

JOHN 15:13

The Bible story in 1 Samuel 18–20 highlights an extraordinary friendship. Jonathan, King Saul's son, had been raised in luxury. Shepherd boy David had spent his time in the fields watching his father's flocks. Theirs was an unlikely pairing, but the Bible says that Jonathan loved David as much as he loved himself.

When King Saul became jealous of David's success, he tried to end David's life. On one occasion when Saul gave orders for David to be killed, Jonathan warned his friend. He then tried to reason with his father, but those efforts were in vain.

Jonathan pledged his loyalty to David: "Whatever you want me to do, I'll do for you" (1 Samuel 20:4), so David and Jonathan hatched a plan. Jonathan would speak to Saul about David, then he'd meet David in a field. If the king had responded favorably, Jonathan would shoot three arrows off to the side, but if David's life was threatened, Jonathan would shoot three arrows beyond his servant boy.

That night, King Saul launched a spear at his son in anger, but Jonathan still risked his life to help his friend. That kind of love, loyalty, and faithfulness is something rare—something we should aim for in our own relationships.

Lord, help me to be a faithful friend.

- How do you feel about the loyalty that Jonathan had for David?
- How is loyalty a continual choice?

Thursday

A Faithful Servant

"But be sure to fear the Lord and serve him faithfully with all
your heart; consider what great things he has done for you."

1 Samuel 12:24

*W*e've seen the blessings of loyalty and faithfulness and how those traits have touched lives, but there are also consequences when those traits are missing.

One day, Sal decided not to go to work because he wanted to see his favorite band play. He reasoned that he didn't have to be faithful, because it was just a job. Sal was a cook at a popular restaurant. When he failed to arrive to prepare the meals, the prep team had to work twice as hard. They did their jobs, but without a chef to run the stove and ovens, only the salads came out of the kitchen! Business people, ready to pay for cooked meals, were turned away hungry and aggravated. The restaurant manager apologized, but many of the customers vowed never to return to such an unreliable establishment.

In his short-sighted disloyalty, Sal had not realized the number of people who relied on his faithfulness in honoring his commitment to his employer.

We all need other people's loyalty, just as much as we benefit from God's faithfulness. Let's purpose in our hearts today that we will be faithful and loyal no matter what we do.

Lord, help me to someday hear you call me a "good and faithful servant" (Matthew 25:21, 23).

- Think about your relationship with God. How do you want to please Him?
- What is one way you can be more faithful in your everyday activities?

33

Writing My Life Story

Moreover it is required in stewards
that one be found faithful.

1 CORINTHIANS 4:2 NKJV

We've learned this week about the positives and negatives of loyalty and faithfulness. We've seen how those traits touched Bob's and Jim's lives, how they played out in Jonathan and David's friendship, and even how fundamental they are to everyday life.

Think about putting these characteristics into practice in your life.

Ask God to open your eyes to the needs of others around you. Our world is filled with people who need someone who will be loyal and faithful in their lives—from the homeless man who needs to know someone cares, to the kid at homeschool co-op who seems like a misfit, to siblings who need to know you have their backs, and, someday, to coworkers or business associates who count on us.

In Hebrews 11, God shares a list of people in the Bible who were found faithful. People like Abel, Noah, Abraham, Sarah, and Moses. Aim for God to someday add your name to that list.

Father, help the traits of loyalty and faithfulness to be so ingrained in my life that they will impact everything that I do.

- Name two people you know who could use someone loyal and faithful in their lives.
- How could you become that person for them?

Annotations

Loyalty and faithfulness are two extraspecial traits—because they imply that God, our family and friends, our fellow students, and our coworkers will know that they can count on us.

....
....
....
....
....
....
....
....
....
....
....
....
....
....
....
....
....
....
....
....
....
....
....
....
....
....

Patience and Self-Restraint

Week
6

Listen Up!

Let every person be quick to hear,
slow to speak, slow to anger.

JAMES 1:19 ESV

We live in a fast-paced world. At every turn we are told, "Hurry up!" Nobody wants to be late or miss anything.

In this verse, though, James encourages us to be quick to listen. We need to be ready to listen with hearts that are available to hear others. This sometimes requires patience.

Often in our conversations, we are too eager to convey our thoughts and words to others, regardless of what they have to say. Sometimes we listen only halfheartedly, mentally planning a response or follow-up story. Being quick to listen is to listen actively, completely focusing on what the other person is communicating.

Being quick to listen also involves self-restraint. We must put aside our own interests and our desire to take center stage in a conversation. Listening to the other people in a conversation lets them know we respect them and that we're interested in what they say and allows us to learn instead of tell. Intent listening, or being quick to listen, shows God's love to those around us.

Lord, help my self-restraint so I put others first in every conversation.

- Why is it challenging to be quick to listen and to be slow when it comes to speaking or becoming angry?
- What is something you deal with every day that requires extra patience?

Worth Waiting For

The end of a matter is better than its beginning,
and patience is better than pride.

ECCLESIASTES 7:8

"*B*ut I want to know now, Mom."

"Lilly, your impatience is not surprising, but I want you to savor the surprise! Just think, next weekend it will be here and you will be so happy!" Lilly's mother smiled knowingly.

The next weekend, Lilly's mom said, "Put on your best dress. We're going to a restaurant, and I want you to look nice."

Lilly shrugged and put on her favorite dress.

Mom and Lilly slipped into their seats in the quiet glow of the evening. As Lilly looked around at the white tabletops with their sparkling glassware and fragrant flowers, a man slid into the seat next to Lilly. He reached over and took Lilly's hand.

"This seat taken?" He smiled at Lilly.

She turned to him, tears in her laughing eyes. "Dad?" He was home from Iraq, and her mom had kept it a surprise.

Being patient is often difficult, especially when we're waiting for God to answer our prayers. However, just as Lilly learned from her mom's surprise, waiting can be a good thing. If we can exercise patience and trust in Him—even when it doesn't make sense to us—we can rest assured that His plan will be worth the wait.

Lord, help me be patient.

- Why is it so difficult to have patience when we're waiting on something?
- How is patience related to humility?

Constantly Building

But let patience have its perfect work, that you
may be perfect and complete, lacking nothing.

JAMES 1:4 NKJV

*B*rad sat on the floor assembling small stones and wood pieces
for the village he was building. He loved the unique features
he could add, but he knew the foundation was most important.
If each piece was not secure in its position, the next pieces could
(and probably would) fall.

Many things in life are similar to Brad's building project. They
are works in progress, and only after securing each foundational
piece can the next level be added. Often we see things we'd like
or qualities we hope to emulate, and sometimes we become impatient because we want things now. Still, just as Brad couldn't rush
the process while building the village, we need to wait on God so
we don't rush His plan for our lives. God will honor our patience
and faithfulness.

If you're in the middle of a crisis and decide you're going to
trust God and read His Word, you are laying a strong foundation
for dealing with your problem. That builds character, which in
turn gives you hope.

Lord, be with me as I build character every day.

- What are some things you are building in your life?
- How has God used things in the past as a foundation
  for what you are doing today?

Waiting with Patience

But you, O Lord, are a God merciful
and gracious, slow to anger and abounding
in steadfast love and faithfulness.

PSALM 86:15 ESV

Joseph was his father's favorite, and Joseph's brothers did not like this. It made them angry, so they threw him into a pit. Some Ishmaelite traders passed by, and his brothers pulled him out and sold him to them. The traders took him to Egypt, where he found favor and became quite successful.

When famine came, Joseph's family needed food. Joseph's treacherous brothers traveled to Egypt in search of sustenance. They found not only food but also their brother (though they didn't recognize him until he told them who he was). Because the king had put Joseph in charge of the grain, he could save his family. Joseph's heart was full of forgiveness for them, and he was excited to be reunited with his family.

Throughout his time in Egypt, Joseph had worked hard and maintained a humble attitude of service to the king. He might justifiably have been angry and bitter about his brothers' betrayal, but instead, he was patient. He prayed fervently and devoted himself fully to his job with the king. As Joseph waited for the desires of his heart, he knew his patient attitude pleased God.

Lord, keep me patient and content during my times of waiting. Help me to remember that you are working on my behalf even when I can't see visible proof.

- What can help you be more patient?
- How is patience the opposite of anger?

Friday

God's Patience

But for that very reason I was shown mercy so that in me,
the worst of sinners, Christ Jesus might display his
immense patience as an example for those who
would believe in him and receive eternal life.

1 TIMOTHY 1:16

This week, we have talked about patience and how to develop that character trait in us. Now think about God's patience.

Obviously, we can't know exactly what God is thinking, but for centuries God has waited for His children to come to Him, and He has resisted wrath toward those who scorn Him.

We know He is coming back. We just don't know when. In His goodness, and because of His patience, it may be quite a while. He loves everyone so much, and He wants the whole world to come to faith in Jesus.

We hear this preached in church. As believers, we have a responsibility to help spread the word to our families, friends, and the world. That kind of ministry requires—you guessed it—patience! In fact, it requires both patience and self-restraint to show others the heart you have for the Lord without making demands on them in return. Share your love for Jesus without asking for anything in return, offering evidence for the joy you carry in your heart.

Lord, help me to share my love with all those around me.

- What was one time you were tempted to be impatient and you prayed for patience?
- When you have Jesus in your heart, is it easier or harder to be patient?

Annotations

Patience and self-restraint don't come easily. Having Jesus in our hearts helps us to serve others with love, grace, and kindness.

....
....
....
....
....
....
....
....
....
....
....
....
....
....
....
....
....
....
....
....
....
....
....
....
....
....
....

Thoroughness and Diligence

Week
7

More Than Just Enough

The plans of the diligent lead to profit
as surely as haste leads to poverty.

PROVERBS 21:5

Imagine visiting the doctor because you're covered in itchy bumps. The doctor glances at you and says, "It's chicken pox." He then walks out the door without another look. That night, however, you end up in the emergency room, where you discover it's a serious allergic reaction. You'd probably be disappointed in your doctor's lack of care. We want our doctors to be thorough and diligent.

Thoroughness is the act of covering every detail, and diligence is earnest and persistent effort. Put together, these traits are powerful characteristics that God recognizes and honors. Being thorough and diligent will make you a better friend, family member, citizen, worshipper—you name it. Possessing these traits shows others they can trust you because you will be persistent in covering every detail.

Many people today do just enough to get by and nothing more, but "just enough" often results in sloppy work. Today's passage says attentiveness leads to profit and hurriedness leads to poverty. As you start this week, stop and ask yourself these questions before completing a task: Did I do my best work? Did I take the time to cover every detail?

Almighty God, inspire me to always do my best.

- How can you be more thorough in one of the many tasks you have each day?
- How can diligence play a role in your spiritual growth?

It's All in the Details

We want each of you to show this same diligence to the
very end, so that what you hope for may be fully realized.

HEBREWS 6:11

*W*hy can moms always find everything? When something
is lost, the first thing you do is ask your mom, and she
responds with, "How hard did you look?" Moms know children
tend to look quickly without lifting, opening, or overturning anything. Instead they're hurried and superficial in their search for
missing items—the exact opposite of thorough and diligent. The
reason you ask your mom is because she embodies thoroughness.

Imagine how crazy your home would be if your parents did
everything hurriedly and superficially. Food might be incom-
pletely cooked, clothes might not be totally clean, or worse,
whites might be washed with reds, irreparably turning them pink.

When traveling, maybe they wouldn't grab enough money to
pay for gas and food because those details would be overlooked.
You may go to the beach without towels, chairs, or sunscreen
because your mom and dad quickly planned and jumped right in
the car. Your days would be fraught with attempts to mitigate the
results of sloppy work, or to make up for poor efforts. Consider
the importance of being comprehensive and attentive.

The strange thing is, when you commit to being more thorough, the task often becomes more enjoyable. Spend a few extra
moments to diligently complete a task, for instance, and your
accomplishment lifts you up in spirit.

God, show me where I need to be more thorough.

- What does "Measure twice, cut once" mean to a carpenter?
- How can you show more diligence in your schoolwork?

Wednesday

Search Diligently

Now finish the work, so that your eager willingness
to do it may be matched by your completion of it,
according to your means.

2 CORINTHIANS 8:11

The roadsides were thick with people who waited on Jesus to pass through the streets of Jericho. Some had heard Him speak before and seen Him perform miracles. Others had only heard of Him but wanted to catch a glimpse.

A tax collector named Zacchaeus was one of those; he wanted to see what the commotion was about. *Who was this man they called the Son of God?* Determined to see Him, the tax collector ran ahead of the crowd. Being shorter than most of the townspeople, Zacchaeus found it necessary to climb up in a tree to see Jesus.

Imagine how Zacchaeus would have missed out if he wasn't diligent or thorough in his search for Jesus. His hunt wasn't easy due to his short stature. When all the people crowded on the street, the wee little man could have stood in the back and pouted. Instead, his diligence paid off. Jesus noticed him and invited him to come down so they could dine together.

Take a few moments right now to consider if you go out of your way to see Jesus, and how you might do so more diligently today than you did yesterday. Plan it right now.

God, let me have the motivation of Zacchaeus when it comes to spending time with you.

- What great things could you be missing because you aren't diligent enough?
- How could you be more diligent in your time alone with God?

Keep Your Eyes Open

Give your complete attention to these matters.
Throw yourself into your tasks so that everyone
will see your progress.

1 TIMOTHY 4:15 NLT

*J*acob was playing in the woods when he tripped and fell on a large tree stump. The stump left a deep gouge, and his mother had to pick the splinters out of his open wound with tweezers. Then she cleaned and bandaged his leg, but that night she didn't have peace about the injury and decided to take him to the doctor. Her fear was confirmed when the doctor sent them for X-rays and found a larger piece of wood deeply embedded into Jacob's shin. The injury required surgery, as well as antibiotics to ensure infection wouldn't set in.

Being thorough saves you from harm in some situations, like getting all the splinters out or making sure the chicken you're having for dinner is thoroughly cooked. It also brings great reward in others, like finding the prize egg in a hunt or making your way to Jesus in a crowd. Whether you're being thorough because of something negative or positive, it always pays to cover every detail. Attention to detail stems from caring about your work. It's a result of true diligence. Do good work to please God and your efforts will not go unnoticed.

Lord, help me to honor you with everything I do.

- What does your schoolwork say about how much you care?
- How does earnest and persistent effort please God?

Your Best Effort

All hard work brings a profit,
but mere talk leads only to poverty.

PROVERBS 14:23

Thoroughness and diligence affect every part of our lives, from finding lost items in the house to completing our school-work on time. Paying attention to detail is also important for our safety, like knowing what to do when we get hurt or how we need to prepare for certain situations. Most important, those traits are closely tied to our spiritual walk with God. Your heavenly Father doesn't force Himself on you. You must choose to spend time with Him, and in the chaos of a busy life, that's not always easy.

Zacchaeus was a grown man who actually climbed a tree to see Jesus. Do you put forth that same amount of effort to get a glimpse of your Savior? The more diligent you are in seeking God's face, the more you will grow in your walk with Him. The more thorough you are in learning to hear and do what He says, the more He will pour out blessings.

Earlier this week, we learned when you are a person who earnestly pays attention to detail, people trust you more. Can God trust you to give your best effort today?

God, multiply my efforts so I'll draw closer to you.

- What comes to mind when you hear about this week's characteristics of thoroughness and diligence?
- How can we use those attributes to further the kingdom of Christ?

Annotations

Thoroughness and diligence are when you persistently cover every detail. These character traits can affect every area of your life.

....
....
....
....
....
....
....
....
....
....
....
....
....
....
....
....
....
....
....
....
....
....
....
....
....

Virtue
and
Purity

Week
8

Following God's Leading

Don't let anyone look down on you because you are young,
but set an example for the believers in speech,
in conduct, in love, in faith and in purity.

1 TIMOTHY 4:12

*E*mily was fifteen years old and had just published her first novel.

"How did you do that?" someone asked.

"I took a writing course to learn how to format the manuscript, then I outlined my story and—"

"No. I mean, you're only fifteen. You just wrote an entire book, and the publisher wants another one already. You have schoolwork, and swimming practice, and so much else."

Emily smiled. "This story has been in my head for a long time. It just kept growing. One day when I was praying, I knew God was telling me it was the right time. So I started writing."

"Didn't you think you should go to college first?"

"I asked God about that. He kept saying, 'Do it now.'"

Emily followed God's leading. She knew she was young but also knew God wanted her to write wholesome material that others her age could relate to. Emily's love for her friends prompted a desire to set a good example with her life and reach many other teens she would never meet.

Lord, help me follow Emily's example of being obedient to you.

- Name three ways you can exemplify virtue to your peers.
- How can someone overcome a fear of being too young?

What's in Your Heart?

It is by his deeds that a lad distinguishes himself
If his conduct is pure and right.

PROVERBS 20:11 NASB

*V*irtue is something that comes from your heart, the very innermost part of who you are. It is an honest pursuit of the good in all dealings. However, some people act impulsively and without considering the effect on others.

For example, last Sunday, Sean's Sunday school teacher was late getting to class. Everyone sat around the table talking, and then the talking escalated to something more like horsing around. As Michael, seated next to Sean, leaned back in his chair, Sean thought it would be really funny to push on the back of the chair just enough to scare Michael. Unfortunately, Michael totally lost his balance and fell backward. His head hit the floor and blood began flowing.

After Michael's trip to the emergency room and six stitches later, Sean realized that his lack of consideration before he acted made him irresponsible and even mean. He knew the other kids often looked to his example, and he regretted his inappropriate and reckless behavior. Then and there, he made a promise to God to use his leadership skills to help others do the right thing instead of to lead them astray.

Lord, instill virtue in my heart so that I will help others see your love.

- How could Sean have acted differently while the class waited for their teacher?
- What often prevents you from choosing the virtuous path?

Wednesday

A Beautiful Gift

But among you there must not be even a hint
of sexual immorality, or of any kind of impurity, or of greed,
because these are improper for God's holy people.

EPHESIANS 5:3

*D*ad pulled out his chair at the table and sat down, placing two gift boxes in front of his two lovely daughters. "Girls, I want to talk to you."

The two young women looked up. "What, Dad?" Sharlynn asked.

"I'm giving each of you a gift. Think about which one you would choose."

Both girls reached for the more beautifully wrapped package. The second box's paper was torn and the box was misshapen. It was not the attractive one.

"Of course," Dad said. "Neither of you want the used, broken-down box. The newer package looks more valuable, doesn't it?"

Kerry looked thoughtful. "What's the point?"

"You are beautiful girls. The world recognizes that, and you will be tempted. However, God's plan is for you to be strong. You need to keep yourselves pure until God sends the mate he has chosen for you. You are His temple and He is living in you."

Both of the girls nodded. "You're right, Dad," Kerry said. "I want to be a beautiful gift for the man God has for me."

Lord, help me remain pure for you.

- Why is purity important?
- What is one way you can show leadership among your peers as you live a life of purity?

Honest Abe

For we aim at what is honorable not only
in the Lord's sight but also in the sight of man.

2 CORINTHIANS 8:21 ESV

Abraham Lincoln, our sixteenth president, was called "Honest Abe." Even though he got the nickname as a young man, it became his campaign slogan when he ran for president of the United States. What an important quality for the president of our country.

As a young man, Lincoln worked as a storekeeper. Once, he discovered he had overcharged a customer by a few cents. He closed the store and walked several miles to return the correct change. Another time he sold a half pound of tea and later discovered the weight on the scale was only a quarter pound. Once again, he closed the store and walked to the customer's house to deliver the additional quarter pound. No amount was too small for Abraham Lincoln to do whatever it took to make it right, because integrity exists in the details.

Even though those incidences occurred when Lincoln was young, he brought his good character into his public adult life. He chose to be a person of honesty because he valued integrity.

It makes God very happy when we copy Lincoln's example and live a pure life filled with integrity.

Lord, help me to live with virtue.

- Describe a time when your character exemplified virtue.
- How does your faith influence you to be virtuous and fair with others?

Your Body—God's Temple

But Daniel resolved that he would not defile himself
with the king's food, or with the wine that he drank.

DANIEL 1:8 ESV

*W*hen King Nebuchadnezzar took over Jerusalem, he ordered a group of young men to be schooled in the palace for three years. Daniel was one of them. Because they were to serve the king, the youths were to be given the same food and wine as the king.

Daniel wanted to eat a healthy diet, one that was properly prepared according to Scripture. He asked the lead steward for special consideration, pleading, "Give us nothing but vegetables to eat and water to drink. Then compare our appearance with that of the young men who eat the royal food, and treat your servants in accordance with what you see" (Daniel 1:12–13).

Initially, the steward refused, but then he allowed Daniel to try it for ten days. At the end of that time, when he compared him with the other young men, those who had followed the vegetable and water diet were much healthier. The steward took all other food away and had all the young men follow Daniel's diet.

Daniel knew that it was better to eat only healthy foods and drink water instead of wine. He adopted a lifestyle of pure eating to honor God. Nutrition is a popular subject today too, but God has always been concerned that we take care of our bodies.

Lord, my body is your temple. Help me to take good care of it.

- Why wasn't Daniel too afraid to ask for special consideration regarding his food?
- How does the way you eat apply to your relationship with God?

Annotations

Virtue and purity are defining aspects of character, reinforcing all other traits like steel bars inside cement. So fill your heart with the things of God.

....
....
....
....
....
....
....
....
....
....
....
....
....
....
....
....
....
....
....
....
....
....
....
....
....
....

Self-Control
and
Self-Discipline

Week
9

Learning a Routine

That each of you should learn to control
your own body in a way that is holy and honorable.

1 THESSALONIANS 4:4

If your brother pulls the chair out from under you, causing you to fall, and you don't jump up and hit him, you are using self-control. When you make the bed after getting up, that's self-discipline. Both characteristics are closely related. Self-control is controlling your emotions, which often, in effect, control your actions. Self-discipline is the process of training yourself to act or behave in a certain way.

Both character traits are important in your spiritual walk. Self-control will help you to respond appropriately to your brother when he annoys you, to change the channel or close the computer browser when something inappropriate is on, and to choose not to talk back in a disrespectful way to your parents. Self-discipline is necessary to make Bible reading and prayer a part of your daily routine.

As you make choices this week, consider whether you are using self-control or self-discipline. Think also about the disciplines you learned as a young child, like washing your hands and praying before meals, and how they've affected who you are today.

Lord, help me to control my emotions and behavior and make them pleasing to you.

- What areas of self-discipline are you working on now?
- How can being disciplined in those areas help you grow in your walk with Christ?

Fighting Temptation

For everything in the world—the lust of the flesh,
the lust of the eyes, and the pride of life—comes not
from the Father but from the world.

1 JOHN 2:16

$\mathcal{M}$any commercials and advertisements are based on the idea of self-indulgence. Ads for cars, food, clothes, and even watches claim they might be expensive, but they will enrich your life. "You deserve it!" and "Treat yourself!" are common themes. Companies know "self" is a powerful motivator.

Jesus provided us with the perfect example of how to combat self-indulgence. After His baptism, He was led into the wilderness by the Holy Spirit, where He had nothing to eat for forty days. Satan tempted Him, telling Him to make food out of stones and throw Himself down from the highest point of the temple to prove He was God's Son. Then satan brought Jesus to a mountaintop, where he showed Him all the world's kingdoms. "'All this I will give you,' he said, 'if you will bow down and worship me'" (Matthew 4:8–9). Jesus used God's Word to respond to satan, and in doing so, He showed us how to fight the temptation to give in to one's self—with Scripture and prayer.

While we aren't perfect as Christ is, we can follow His leading in responding to the evil one and the temptations of this world.

Heavenly Father, may I always turn to you when I'm tempted to give in to my own selfish desires.

- What are some verses you could memorize to help combat temptation?
- What advertisements use self-indulgence to sell their products? Have you fallen prey to any of them?

Snack Attack

For the Spirit God gave us does not make us timid,
but gives us power, love and self-discipline.

2 TIMOTHY 1:7

*E*ver been "hangry"? It's an emotion felt when you are so hungry, you're angry. Strong emotions often cause a lack of self-control. Don't believe it? Go to the grocery store when you're hungry and you'll be likely to fill your cart with everything you see. Likewise, when you speak out of anger, you may regret the things you say.

Esau may have been "hangry" in the story we find in Genesis 25 where he is tricked by his brother, Jacob. Esau came in from the field famished and asked Jacob for some of the stew he was cooking. Jacob told his brother he would trade him stew for his birthright, as Esau was the older of the two and was due a larger inheritance and blessing. In his hunger, Esau lacked self-control and eagerly traded.

Learning to control your emotions, whether extreme happiness, sorrow, hunger, or even envy, leads to making wiser decisions and better behavior. In this story, if Esau had the self-discipline to carry a snack to the field, he may have had more self-control because his hunger wouldn't have been as strong.

Lord, help me to practice self-control when emotions get the best of me.

- What specific self-disciplines can you practice that will in turn help you to use self-control?
- How did Esau's lack of self-discipline and self-control affect the rest of his life?

Consequences of Sin

Like a city whose walls are broken through
is a person who lacks self-control.

PROVERBS 25:28

The Israelites, following Joshua's lead, successfully brought down the walls of Jericho. Before they did, the Lord warned Joshua that the men were not to take any of the silver or gold, for it was to be devoted to the Lord and go into His treasury. Following that triumph in Jericho, Joshua sent a smaller group to conquer the people of Ai, knowing they would claim victory because the Lord was on their side. Imagine Joshua's surprise when the men of Ai killed thirty-six of the Israelites and sent them running back.

When Joshua questioned God, the Almighty revealed that someone in the camp had lacked self-control and taken items devoted to God. After Joshua went through each of the tribes and families, the Lord revealed that Achan was the guilty individual. Achan then admitted that he kept a beautiful robe, a bar of gold, and some silver. To purge the camp of Achan's sin against God, Achan and his family were stoned, and all his property was destroyed.

Lack of self-control brings consequences that affect all those around us. Sin never stops with just one person; its impact touches many.

God, make me aware of the extreme cost and consequence of choosing myself over you.

- When was one time that the consequences of your lack of self-control caused others to suffer as well?
- Why do you think God allowed Achan's family to be killed along with him?

Keep up the Good Work

Fools give full vent to their rage,
but the wise bring calm in the end.

PROVERBS 29:11

*N*ehemiah was given the task of rebuilding the walls of Jerusalem. After organizing the workers and starting reconstruction, a leader from the area named Sanballet, and one of his friends, Tobiah, did everything they could to discourage the work. They made fun of the men. They scoffed at the wall, telling the workers a fox could knock it down. Day after day they tossed insults toward the men on the wall.

You can imagine their words made Nehemiah and the other Jews angry. Instead of responding in wrath, though, they calmly continued their work. When Sanballet realized his taunts were ineffective, he crafted a second, more devious plot to obstruct progress on the wall, and genially pressed Nehemiah to come down and talk to him. Displaying incredible self-control and self-discipline, Nehemiah simply continued laboring.

When people say things about us that aren't true, often our first instinct is to defend ourselves and respond in the same unkind way. However, if we are self-disciplined enough to stay in God's Word, He will grant us the self-control to respond in a Christlike way.

God, when people trigger my emotions with insults, help me to look to you instead of responding in anger.

- When was a time you struggled to be kind when someone said mean or untrue things about you?
- How are self-discipline and self-control closely linked? Which usually comes first?

Annotations

Self-control deals with emotions while self-discipline is connected to behavior. When you have the discipline to read God's Word and spend time in prayer, God will give you self-control.

Discernment and Discrimination

Week
10

Practicing Discernment

It is the glory of God to conceal a matter;
to search out a matter is the glory of kings.

PROVERBS 25:2

*M*arianna was captain of the soccer team and well respected by her teammates. During one game, a teammate stepped out of bounds. The referees called it good, but Marianna was sitting on the sidelines and had a better view of the play. She knew her teammate had stepped out of bounds, and yet the ref called the play good, which resulted in a goal. Marianna knew she had to speak up and let the referees know what she had seen.

The book of Proverbs tells us kings must use discernment and discrimination, but this instruction applies to us all. No matter what our age or position, we need discernment and discrimination to make good decisions.

The places you need such discernment might be at a sports game, at school, or in your own home. You may have to discern whether a new person you meet would make a good friend or not, or whether to go to a certain party.

Discernment often is a matter of the heart. God will give you the wisdom you need to make good judgments, but as the Scripture says, we must search out matters ourselves and discover the different values inherent in our choices.

Lord, help me to make good choices with your help.

- What are two ways to exercise discernment and good discrimination?
- How can you prepare for times when you need good discernment?

We Are One

My brothers and sisters, believers in our glorious
Lord Jesus Christ must not show favoritism.
Suppose a man comes into your meeting wearing a gold ring
and fine clothes, and a poor man in filthy old clothes also
comes in. If you show special attention to the man wearing
fine clothes and say, "Here's a good seat for you,"
but say to the poor man, "You stand there" or
"Sit on the floor by my feet," have you not discriminated
among yourselves and become judges with evil thoughts?

JAMES 2:1–4

People may look different, but deep down inside, all people are alike. Every person has a heart with the capacity to love, which has nothing to do with looks. Every person wants to love and be loved.

How do you look at those around you? Do you look at their appearance, or do you see them as God's children who need love and acceptance?

Don't choose your friends by how they look. Approach them as your sisters and brothers whom God loves greatly. Try to understand their hearts and discern if they are trustworthy, loyal, and honoring of God. This is the true test of friendship, because you must be diligent in not allowing yourself to be led astray.

Lord, let me show your love to everyone.

- Discrimination can be a good thing or a bad thing. Give an example of each.
- When have you used discernment to honor God?

What Does That Mean?

I am your servant; give me discernment
that I may understand your statutes.

PSALM 119:125

*K*ing David has been called a man after God's own heart. Wouldn't that be a wonderful thing for your friends to say about you? David realized that he had no wisdom or discernment apart from God's direction. He completely trusted God to give him understanding. David spent a lot of time talking to God and asking Him for discernment. He wanted to know God's mind and heart—and that would be a great thing for us to seek after as well.

Has your mom or dad ever told you something and it just didn't make sense to you? As hard as you tried, you couldn't understand the meaning of what they said. What did you do? You asked them to clarify what they were saying so you could completely understand.

Sometimes when we read our Bibles, we may, like David, have to ask for discernment and clarification. We should ask God to open our mind and heart to clearly understand the messages He has for us. That is one of the reasons why God sent His Holy Spirit—to interpret His Word in our hearts and to give us understanding and discernment.

Lord, I need your discernment. Help me to know your heart and mind.

- Tell of one experience when you knew God's Holy Spirit gave you discernment.
- Name two ways you can tell if God is speaking to you.

Thursday

Dress with Modesty

*I also want the women to dress modestly, with decency
and propriety, adorning themselves, not with elaborate
hairstyles or gold or pearls or expensive clothes.*

1 TIMOTHY 2:9

*S*hea came down the steps.

"Have a good time, honey," Dad said. "You look so pretty and … Wait. Where are you going in that outfit? You couldn't possibly sit down in that skirt."

She looked down at her clothes. "But, Dad, everyone will laugh at me if I wear a long skirt."

"You don't have to wear a long skirt, just a longer one. Honey, you don't realize it, but a skirt like that will have all the boys at the dance staring. You are showing more of your body than necessary. You are a beautiful girl. There is a way of dressing with decency."

"But all the girls—"

"You know it doesn't matter what *all the girls* are doing. We want you to understand that your body is a temple of God and you must take good care of it. Dressing modestly is part of that. A big part."

Shea nodded. "Okay, Dad. I guess I'll go change."

Sometimes it's hard not to want to go along with the crowd, but part of being modest includes knowing and doing the right thing. Exercising discrimination in your fashion choices pleases God.

Lord, help me honor your temple.

- Why is dressing modestly important?
- What does how you choose to look on the outside say about what's on the inside?

Sharing God's Love

Hiram king of Tyre replied by letter to Solomon:
"Because the Lord loves his people, he has made you their
king." And Hiram added: "Praise be to the Lord, the God of
Israel, who made heaven and earth! He has given King David
a wise son, endowed with intelligence and discernment, who
will build a temple for the Lord and a palace for himself."

2 CHRONICLES 2:11–12

*K*ing Hiram recognized that God had sent a wise leader. Solomon, David's son, shared his father's wisdom, intelligence, and discernment. Can you imagine how much discernment a king would need?

In today's news, when we hear of kings, presidents, and heads of other countries, we don't necessarily use the same words to describe them as were used back in biblical times. Even so, their needs for those traits today are the same as they were centuries ago.

Just as Solomon was building a temple for God, we are also helping to build His kingdom here on earth. We are His representatives and must do our best to introduce others to Him through His Son Jesus Christ. Through the Holy Spirit, we can find the discernment to understand how best to share the love of Jesus with those who cross our paths. After all, every person we meet presents an opportunity.

Lord, thank you for giving me discernment and discrimination to know the right thing to do.

- What happened the last time you acted rashly, before using discernment?
- What is one area of your life where you are going to try to be more discerning?

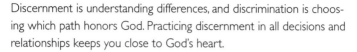

Annotations

Discernment is understanding differences, and discrimination is choosing which path honors God. Practicing discernment in all decisions and relationships keeps you close to God's heart.

....
....
....
....
....
....
....
....
....
....
....
....
....
....
....
....
....
....
....
....
....
....
....

Determination and Drive

Week
11

I'm Going to Do That!

Therefore I do not run like someone running aimlessly;
I do not fight like a boxer beating the air. No, I strike a blow
to my body and make it my slave so that after I have preached
to others, I myself will not be disqualified for the prize.

1 CORINTHIANS 9:26–27

Trent was in awe as he watched the Olympic track and field events. A dream was planted in his young heart that day. He went online and found tips for how to train at home, and first thing the next morning, he started running. Some God-given talent was already there, but now he added drive and determination to the mix.

People chuckled when he told them he was going to be an Olympian, but he said, "I'm going to be on the podium one day accepting my gold medal."

Folks expected him to quit after a few days, but much like England's famous Eddie the Eagle, his passion created an unrelenting, driving force. Trent's dedication paid off the day he stepped down from the podium with a gold medal around his neck.

Imagine what we could do for God if we had that same kind of drive and determination, if we'd serve Him so well that He could someday place a crown of righteousness on our heads.

Lord, help me to run the race of life with determination and drive.

- Why do some people make it to the Olympics and others don't?
- How can that apply to you spiritually?

Racing toward the Prize

I press toward the goal for the prize of
the upward call of God in Christ Jesus.

<small>PHILIPPIANS 3:14 NKJV</small>

Trent never lost sight of the goal. He often sacrificed to become the best—getting up early to exercise, missing events because he prioritized his training, working when he didn't feel well or when his body ached. While everyone else was out having fun, he consistently strove to reach his goal.

That kind of drive and dedication is inspiring, but what if he hadn't done that? What if, instead, he'd been fainthearted and lazy? What if he'd decided it would be okay to miss some practices or turn his alarm off and sleep through his morning workouts?

Most of us aren't training for a track and field event, but we are training for the tasks God has for us to do. We can learn a valuable lesson from Trent's determination and drive, because if we're lazy and don't learn what God wants us to learn each day, and if we don't spend time with Him, we won't be strong and equipped to serve Him. As Trent understood, it's committing to consistently do our best that can make a real difference—even if it's just applying ourselves to the classwork that we really don't want to do.

Lord, make me strong so I can serve you.

- How can you improve your determination each day?
- How can someone cultivate "drive" in themselves?

I'm Not Quitting!

Do you not know that in a race all the runners run,
but only one gets the prize?
Run in such a way as to get the prize.

1 CORINTHIANS 9:24

*A*ll of us have heard the story of Noah and the ark, but consider what it must have been like for him during the ark-building process. Imagine the conversation when he told his wife what he was going to do. Other people likely thought he was an idiot when he started building an enormous boat. They made fun of him, but he didn't let the peer pressure stop him. The ark was huge and it took a long, backbreaking process to build it. Noah could have quit at any time, but he was determined to fulfill what God had asked him to do.

Contemplate the drive of Trent and Noah. It's not sufficient to simply recognize what God wants for your life; it's necessary to exercise the discipline required to achieve it. That's where determination and choosing excellence comes in. If pleasing God is the ultimate goal, and it is because of who He is, then nothing should be able to deter you from attaining it. Don't stand before Him someday knowing that you didn't run the race well.

Lord, help me to serve you faithfully each day—to keep my eye on the prize.

- What are some personal goals you'd like to set?
- What are some spiritual goals you'd like to set?

Becoming the Best

And let us not grow weary while doing good,
for in due season we shall reap if we do not lose heart.

GALATIANS 6:9 NKJV

The first thing Trent had to do when he began his journey to become a world-class runner was to set a goal. If we don't have goals, we have nothing to aim toward—and nothing to achieve. Success doesn't happen by accident.

Lots of people want to make the track team or be an Olympian, but very few people actually accomplish that, because they lack the drive and determination that would fuel their passion. When the first discouraging moment comes along, they quit. Either they aren't willing to put the effort into it that it requires, or they lack the faith that any difficult endeavor demands.

Becoming the best often means leaving your comfort zone, and being willing to fail, despite tremendous effort. That's where a belief and reliance on God steadies you.

A coach doesn't want a quitter on his team, and God doesn't need one on His team either. Think about the fact that *you* are on God's team and that He's counting on you. By determining to be faithful in little things, you build strength to achieve big goals.

Father, help me to set huge goals for you.

- Is it better to listen to God or to other people when it comes to your goals?
- Why do people quit when the going gets tough?

Finishing Well

I have fought the good fight, I have finished the course,
I have kept the faith.

2 TIMOTHY 4:7 NASB

*D*rive and determination paid off for Trent when he became a champion athlete. It paid off for Noah when he fulfilled the task God gave him, and he and his family were safe during the flood.

Those traits can do the same for you. God has a plan and a purpose for each of us. He's given you unique talents, skills, and life experiences. Just as each snowflake is different, every one of us is a one-of-a-kind design and purpose. If you become lazy or complacent, you won't accomplish the tasks He has for you. They'll be left undone, or for someone else to fulfill for God.

Sometimes that happens because of fear of failure. However, when Michael Jordan was asked how he became the greatest basketball player, he answered that he failed a lot. There is satisfaction in knowing that we tried, and there is a determination to succeed that is fueled by failure. God doesn't call us to a task without providing all we need to perform it. Listen diligently to the encouragement of God, not to the discouragement of others, and master your determination to fulfill the plans God has for you.

Father, give me the drive to step out in faith, and determination to push for success.

- What holds people back from reaching their goals?
- How can you increase your determination to accomplish something?

Annotations

Drive and determination are the fuel behind our ambitions. They are important traits that we need to achieve God's purposes for us.

....
....
....
....
....
....
....
....
....
....
....
....
....
....
....
....
....
....
....
....
....
....
....
....
....

Enthusiasm
and
Joyfulness

Week
12

Cleaning up Our Attitudes

Never be lazy, but work hard
and serve the Lord enthusiastically.

ROMANS 12:11 NLT

When Amanda and Michael finished their schoolwork, their mom said, "I want you to clean your rooms. Straighten up the mess, make your beds, dust, clean the mirrors, and then vacuum. And when you finish that, straighten up your closets. Do a good job."

Michael answered, "Okay, Mom." He whistled while he worked, enthusiastically pushing the vacuum across the carpet. He polished the mirror and furniture until they gleamed. He had joy in doing a good job, in pleasing his mom. His room looked great.

Amanda, on the other hand, grumbled and griped her way through the afternoon. She had no enthusiasm for the task, and it showed in the crooked bedspread, haphazard cleaning job, and pile of items that she tried to hide in the corner of the closet— her idea of straightening up the mess.

Not many people look forward to cleaning tasks, but enthusiasm made Michael's afternoon a pleasurable experience. Amanda's attitude made for a miserable day—especially after she got in trouble because she didn't complete her assigned task.

God wants us to serve Him with enthusiasm and joy. Do you need to add "clean up your attitude" to *your* to-do list today?

Lord, give me a joyful heart in all that I do.

- What can we learn from Michael's and Amanda's attitudes?
- How do enthusiasm and joyfulness apply to us spiritually?

Contagious Joy

And whatever you do, in word or deed,
do everything in the name of the Lord Jesus,
giving thanks to God the Father through him.

COLOSSIANS 3:17 ESV

*H*ave you ever been around someone who was sick with the flu and you caught what they had? They were *contagious*. Your attitude can also be contagious. Think about when you've been with someone who was happy and excited. That kind of joy usually spreads to everyone in the room.

Grumpiness sometimes seems to be even more contagious than joy. If you ever had one family member who was grouchy, within a few hours, that gloom has likely affected the whole family, ruining the time for everyone. Even more importantly, they've grieved God's heart because *their* heart attitude has been wrong. Often, that bad attitude was caused by something that wasn't even important in the first place.

It doesn't have to be like that. Your attitude is your choice, even when someone else is trying to make you feel differently. Choose to be joyful, though, and you may just turn someone else's day around. Determine today that you'll choose joy instead of being grouchy and that you'll serve God and others with enthusiasm and kindness. Experiment today with infecting people around you with your joy.

Father, help my heart and attitude to please you. Give me a spirit of joyfulness that is contagious to everyone around me.

- How can you try to spread joy to those around you?
- How can we change our attitudes?

Wednesday

Singing in the Dark

But at midnight Paul and Silas were praying and singing
hymns to God, and the prisoners were listening to them.

ACTS 16:25 NKJV

*I*f ever two people had reason to be grouchy and mad, Paul
and Silas were those men. Acts 16 tells the story of how a
magistrate convicted them unlawfully. An angry crowd attacked
them, and they were beaten severely with rods before they were
thrown into a dank and depressing prison cell. Their feet were
even locked down in stocks so they couldn't move around.

For most of us, anger and self-pity would have ruled the night.
Paul and Silas, however, did something amazing, instead. At midnight, when they were surrounded by darkness both physical and
emotional, as they sat there in great pain, they prayed and sang
praises to God with such enthusiasm that the other prisoners
heard them. They shared joy. I'm sure that wasn't the norm there,
and one can only imagine how strange it was to hear singing in a
dank, decaying prison where there was normally just gloom and
despair.

Because of how Paul and Silas reacted to the situation, the
light of Jesus infiltrated that prison, bringing hope to men who
moments before had been hopeless, and joy to where heartache
once ruled.

Father, give me joy even in the midst of difficult circumstances.

- How do you respond when something bad happens to
  you?
- How does God want you to respond?

Choices and Consequences

Be joyful in hope, patient in affliction, faithful in prayer.
ROMANS 12:12

*M*ichael cleaned his room with enthusiasm, and he found joy in doing a good job. Amanda had just the opposite approach. Her negative attitude and self-pity because she didn't want to clean made a bad situation worse, and there were consequences: she wasted the time that she should have been cleaning, she had to to go back and do the job right anyway, and she wasn't allowed to go out with her friends later. She disappointed her mom, and her poor attitude made their home an unpleasant place that afternoon. It was a hard lesson to learn, but after that, whenever her mom asked for her help, Amanda made much wiser choices.

Paul and Silas also had a choice to make when they were condemned to a depressing prison cell. They could have become bitter at God, and they could have sat there wallowing in self-pity. Instead, they *chose* to continue serving Him with joy and enthusiasm, despite their horrible, desperate circumstances. They discovered that joy, enthusiasm, and prayer makes a powerful combination.

Because of that decision, other lives were changed for eternity. That's why choosing enthusiasm and joyfulness is important for us as well, because others are listening and watching us to see how we live each day.

Lord, help me to choose joy in every circumstance.

- What adjustments can you make to have a steadily positive attitude?
- How is joyfulness a choice?

Friday

A Dose of Joy

A joyful heart is good medicine.
PROVERBS 17:22 NASB

This week we've seen the positive benefits of enthusiasm and joy. We've seen the consequences when grumpiness and self-pity move in. Now it's time to put what we've learned into action. Our verse today says, "A joyful heart is good medicine," so let's offer a dose of joy to others.

There are some practical ways to do that. Call someone and offer encouragement. Everyone wants to know that somebody cares. Pay a visit to some elderly neighbors. Sometimes older people go for days without seeing another person. Your smiling face might be the best medicine they'll get that day. Offer to do some simple chores to help them.

Ask your mom or dad what you can do to help them—without even being asked! Then do it enthusiastically and with joy. Experiment with saying something nice (Gasp!) to your siblings. Give them a sincere compliment. They might not say so, but it will mean the world to them.

Along the way, you're going to make an amazing discovery—because you'll find that whenever you give joyously, somehow *you* are the one who gets tremendous blessings and joy.

Lord, thank you for joy. Help me to share that with others.

- What are three ways that you can bless someone this week?
- How do you feel when someone does something nice for you?

Annotations

Choosing enthusiasm and joyfulness can affect every aspect of our lives—and the lives of others. When we give joy away, it always comes back to us in bigger portions.

. . . .

. . . .

. . . .

. . . .

. . . .

. . . .

. . . .

. . . .

. . . .

. . . .

. . . .

. . . .

. . . .

. . . .

. . . .

. . . .

. . . .

. . . .

. . . .

. . . .

. . . .

. . . .

. . . .

. . . .

. . . .

. . . .

Humility and Humor

Week
13

Knock, Knock!

"He will yet fill your mouth with laughter
and your lips with shouts of joy."

JOB 8:21

Stan Laurel and Oliver Hardy were a comedic duo during the classic Hollywood era. They became famous for slapstick comedy, where they weren't afraid to look silly for a laugh. Like Laurel and Hardy, this week's character qualities go hand in hand—humility and humor.

A recent study by the University of California at Berkeley connected the ability to laugh at oneself with greater health benefits.* Participants were shown distorted pictures of strangers and asked to rate the level of humor in each. Within those photos was a distorted picture of each of the participants as well. As those in the study saw their own photos, most smiled and laughed. Cameras captured and analyzed their expressions, determining how genuine they were. Were they truly able to find humor in their own silly photos? The study found that those who genuinely laughed at themselves were overall more cheerful and less dour.

God gave us the ability to laugh for a reason. It's fun, and it's good for us. As you start this week, when you find yourself in a humbling situation, look for humor. When you face hardship, find a way to smile. You will feel better. No joke.

God, help me not to take myself so seriously, and grant me the ability to laugh at myself.

- Describe the last time you laughed at yourself.
- Why is humility such an important part of humor?

---

* Rita Rubin, "Can You Laugh at Yourself? Scientists Put Laughter to the Test," *NBC News*, July 26, 2011, http://bodyodd.nbcnews.com/_news/2011/07/26/7143331-can-you-laugh-at-yourself-scientists-put-humor-to-the-test.

Tuesday

Up and Down

When pride comes, then comes disgrace,
but with humility comes wisdom.

PROVERBS 11:2

*H*ave you ever seen someone become angry over making a hilarious mistake? Instead of admitting their fault and laughing at the gaffe, they angrily point fingers and place blame on anyone but themselves.

Pride, the exact opposite of humility, is limiting. Pride is the process of lifting oneself up, while humility is lifting up others. When people become prideful, they prefer playing the blame game to admitting their own shortcoming. We are humans and are bound to make mistakes on a daily, sometimes hourly, basis. How we react when we fail is our choice.

Often too much pride indicates insecurity. When you lack self-confidence, you have the need to continually lift yourself up. However, when you are self-assured, you own up to your flaws and even find the hilarity in your mistakes, recognizing that it doesn't make you less of a person to admit your weaknesses.

Christ is the perfect example of someone who was strong but not afraid to be humble. He even lowered himself enough to wash the disciples' feet. True strength comes from humility, and in that humility, God often provides comic relief.

Lord, remove my pride and help me live with humility.

- Why do you think it's easier to laugh at yourself about some things and not about others?
- In what areas do you struggle to show humility?

Donkey Talk

"For all those who exalt themselves will be humbled,
and those who humble themselves will be exalted."

LUKE 14:11

Sometimes God teaches humility in a humorous way—and one of those stories is found in Numbers 22. Balaam had the gift of divination. Balak, the king of Moab, sent messengers to ask him to curse the Israelites. The Lord told Balaam the Israelites were blessed and not to harm them—but when Balaam relayed this message to Balak, the king rejected that answer and demanded Balaam come see him.

When Balaam set off on his donkey, God was displeased and placed an angel with a sword in the middle of the road. Balaam couldn't see him, but his donkey could and refused to move. The diviner beat his donkey for not moving, until the donkey said, "What have I done to you to make you beat me these three times?" (Numbers 22:28).

Balaam had a full conversation with the donkey before God allowed him to see the heavenly being in the road. Upon seeing the angel, Balaam immediately humbled himself and confessed his sin. The angel warned him to speak only the words God would give.

Imagine carrying on a conversation with a donkey! While humbling at first, Balaam probably laughed about it later.

God, thank you for using humor to teach humility. Open my eyes to always see you.

- When has God used humor to teach you a lesson?
- Why would God use a donkey to speak to Balaam?

A Prescription for Laughter

Our mouths were filled with laughter,
our tongues with songs of joy.

PSALM 126:2

"*L*aughter is the best medicine" is a popular saying because there is truth to it. People with a positive attitude who laugh frequently are often healthier. Bitterness or lack of humor is linked to ulcers and depression. The Berkeley study mentioned earlier in the week revealed that the ability to laugh at yourself makes for greater health benefits. Imagine a life without humor: no knock, knock jokes; no April Fool's hilarity, no silly dance moves or inside jokes with your best friends. It's nearly inconceivable.

Humor is terribly useful. It can open the door to relationships, both personal and business. God used it with Balaam to get his attention and bring him to humility. Comedy can help people relax and get their minds off the problems of the day. In hospitals, clowns endeavor to make sick children laugh because the laughter releases endorphins that relieve pain.

Think about how humor is typically an unexpected outcome. Some people don't like surprises, though, and struggle to wee what's funny in many jokes. Take note today of every time you laugh and why, and thank God for a sense of security and the gift of humor.

Thank you, God, for laughter, and that something so fun to do can be so good for me.

- What things make you laugh the most?
- Why do you think some people become bitter and don't often laugh?

Invitation to Giggle

A time to weep and a time to laugh,
a time to mourn and a time to dance.

Ecclesiastes 3:4

*K*ing Solomon said there is a time for everything—even a time to laugh. We've learned this week how humor and humility go hand in hand. We must be humble enough to see our own flaws and find humor in them. Laughter is important. It keeps us healthy, and it keeps us humble. Those who can learn to laugh at themselves are more confident individuals, and people are often drawn to them. Think about your friends. Are you more drawn to the ones with a great sense of humor who are also humble enough to serve others?

Do you have some friends or people you know who could use a good laugh? Perhaps they are going through a period of disquiet or despondency. Invite them over for a family game night or maybe a youth activity at your church. Maybe your family could plan a visit to a retirement center where there are some senior citizens who could use a good laugh. Smiles are free, and the more you give them away, the more you get in return.

Lord, show me someone who needs the gift of laughter, and open the doors for me to share with them.

- What things can you do to bring more humor into your own life?
- Imagine life without humor and then life without humility. Which would be more of a struggle and why?

Annotations

Humor and humility go hand in hand. Learning not to take yourself so seriously is a great way to laugh and to learn from your mistakes.

....
....
....
....
....
....
....
....
....
....
....
....
....
....
....
....
....
....
....
....
....
....
....
....
....
....

Faith and Prayerfulness

Week
14

Faith Like a Little Child

"And whatever things you ask in prayer,
believing, you will receive."

MATTHEW 21:22 NKJV

Seven-year-old Jeremy watched in horror as his beloved puppy, Waggie-Tail, fell off a steep bank and landed on packed dirt twenty feet below. Tears sprang to his eyes as the puppy lay sprawled there, motionless. His parents heard Jeremy's yell for help, and they rushed to see what was wrong. They prepared a soft bed and moved the dog to the quiet basement. Hours went by and the puppy just lay there.

At dinner that night, Jeremy prayed, "Dear Jesus, please help Waggie-Tail to get better. Amen." The minute he finished praying, he jumped up from the table and ran to the basement door. When his mother asked where he was going, he said, "I prayed. Waggie-Tail is going to be better." He was.

Now that's faith. Jeremy discovered something that many of us forget: Faith and prayer go together just as naturally as peanut butter and jelly, and one doesn't work without the other. Faith is believing in something we can't see. Otherwise, it's not faith. As well, when we add a heaping helping of faith to our prayers, we have something that's way more powerful than any superhero.

Father, give me faith to trust you even when I can't see the answer. Thank you for hearing and answering my prayers.

- What can we learn from this little boy's faith?
- How do faith and prayerfulness go together?

Mustard Seed Faith

Now faith is the substance of things hoped for,
the evidence of things not seen.

HEBREWS 11:1 NKJV

If we lack faith we perceive things through the filter of what *we* can do, instead of recognizing God's limitless resources and abilities.

Faith is believing in something we haven't seen. If a problem is something we can fix ourselves, we don't need faith when we pray about it. However, when it's a huge, seemingly insurmountable problem, something that appears hopeless, we call on our faith in our great and gracious God to pull us through. That's where our prayers get serious, and that's where we truly begin to trust God. Abe Lincoln said he often was driven to his knees when he realized he had no place else to go.

To Jeremy, it was a big deal when his puppy was injured, but what was so cool about his story was that after Jeremy's prayer, he *expected* Waggie-Tail to be better when he went to check on him. As a result, God honored that little boy's faith.

God tells us some awesome things in the Bible about prayer and faith. He gives the example of a mustard seed. Have you ever seen one? They're just tiny specks, but God says that if we have even that amount of faith when we pray, we can move mountains.

Lord, give me a faith that's bigger than mustard seeds. Help me to believe you will answer my prayers.

- How often do you really believe that God will answer your prayers?
- Why might we struggle with having or keeping faith?

Rhoda's Prayer Group

That your faith should not be in
the wisdom of men but in the power of God.

1 CORINTHIANS 2:5 NKJV

*D*o you remember the story in Acts 12 where King Herod put Peter into prison? Herod delighted in persecuting believers. He ordered four squads of four soldiers to guard Peter. Even when he slept, Peter was chained between two soldiers, with another guarding the gate. Herod certainly didn't mean for him to go anywhere. Meanwhile, at Mary's house, the church prayed earnestly that God would deliver Peter.

While they were praying, God sent an angel to awaken Peter. The chains fell from his wrists and the angel told him to get dressed. Yes, God sprung Peter from the prison.

Peter headed straight to Mary's house, where prayers for him were still in progress. When he knocked on the door, the young girl, Rhoda, who answered it, was so excited she didn't even open the door and just left him standing there while she ran to share the news: "Peter is at the door!" (Acts 12:14). They didn't believe her and were amazed when they saw him standing there.

Yes, they'd prayed, but they lacked the faith and trust that God would answer their prayers. We often do the exact same thing.

Father, when I pray, give me faith to believe.

- Discuss a time when you prayed and then you were surprised when God answered.
- What is one way you can increase your faith?

Worse Than a Scary Movie

And whatever you ask in My name, that I will do,
that the Father may be glorified.

JOHN 14:13 NKJV

*C*an you imagine being unable to talk to God? The thought of that is worse than any scary movie. God is our constant, immutable source of strength, our go-to person in our times of need. We ought to pray so much and so often that prayerfulness becomes a way of life for us, so we must have faith that God can handle whatever we send His way.

Faith is like a chair. When you start your school day, do you stop and examine the chair to make sure it will hold you? No, you just mindlessly plop down on the seat without even thinking about it. Why? Because you've sat in that chair many times before and it's always held you without any problem.

It's the same way with prayer. There are so many stories recorded in the Bible of God's faithfulness, we should disallow any aberrant misgivings or doubt. Strive to have faith to believe that the God who has taken care of us in the past will remain committed to us in the future. Rely on Him. After all, there's not one verse in the Bible that says, "And then God failed me."

God, thank you so much for the gift of prayer. Use my faith and prayer life to glorify you.

° What can a chair teach us about faith?
° Why is prayer often our last resort instead of our first?

Faith That Soars

But without faith it is impossible to please Him.

HEBREWS 11:6 NKJV

We've learned about a little boy who had faith when he prayed for his injured puppy, and we've talked about some adults who prayed earnestly for Peter's release but didn't really believe that God would answer their prayers. In both of those examples prayer, and its effectiveness, was tested and proven, regardless of the faith of those praying.

For young Jeremy, his faith was strong before he opened the basement door and saw his puppy standing at the bottom of the stairs with bright eyes and a tail that wagged back and forth like a conductor's baton at a fast symphony. He received visual proof that God rewarded his faith and answered his prayers.

For Peter's prayer group, their faith in an awesome God was rewarded when their prayers were met despite their doubt. Imagine their awe as Peter shared how God had sent an angel to break his chains. Perhaps they felt guilty for doubting God, but surely the next time they prayed, they did so with new levels of faith and fervor.

Remind yourself of the times God recognized your heart's desires. Use them to bolster your faith and bring glory to God by sharing your stories of how He's honored your faith with answered prayers.

God, give me faith that soars and keep me ever prayerful.

- How can you encourage someone else's faith?
- How do you keep faithful even through seemingly unanswered prayers?

Annotations

Faith and prayerfulness are so intertwined that you can't have one without the other. Put them to use in your life, and watch some amazing things happen.

Thankfulness
and
Appreciation

Week
15

Monday

A Thankful Heart

Oh give thanks to the Lord, for He is good.

PSALM 107:1 NASB

Ted and John went shoe shopping with their dad, Keith. Basketball season had arrived, and both boys had outgrown their sports shoes.

Keith had worked a lot of overtime lately to provide for his family, sometimes until late in the evening. John noticed his dad's exhaustion, so he planned to find some inexpensive shoes when they went shopping. Instead, his dad said, "I never had nice shoes when I was growing up. Just this once, I want you boys to get whatever brand of sneakers you want. Don't worry about the cost."

Ted just shrugged. Parents were *supposed* to buy shoes for their kids, so it was no big deal to him. He didn't even say thank you.

John saw the effort that went into that moment. He chose a pair of good shoes that he didn't feel were overpriced and said sincerely, "Dad, thank you so much for my shoes. I know how many hours you worked to buy them, and I really appreciate it."

God wants us to have a grateful spirit like John's—one that appreciates the sacrifice and love that accompanies our blessings—and since we celebrate Thanksgiving this week, it would be a perfect time to thank God for His amazing goodness to us.

Father, give me a thankful heart.

- What can you do to have a more thankful heart?
- Who do you need to thank today and for what?

A Gift from My Father

Every good and perfect gift is from above,
coming down from the Father of the heavenly lights,
who does not change like shifting shadows.

JAMES 1:17

If you do something nice for people, do you want them to just take it for granted, or do you want them to notice and to express their thanks? There's something in all of us that wants to be appreciated. I'm sure Keith was touched when his son John expressed his gratitude in a manner that showed he genuinely appreciated his father's sacrifice and love.

What about Ted's reaction? Ted didn't even say thank you because he felt *entitled* to have the best basketball shoes and whatever else was given to him. Ted's ungrateful heart was a disappointment to his father, and it took some joy out of buying the shoes for him.

There is a vast difference between giving thanks and having gratitude. Gratitude is predominantly inward. We may be grateful for our blessings without ever acknowledging their source. Thankfulness compels an action—to give thanks to others and to God.

Just as Keith found joy in John's thankful heart, God takes delight in hearing our praise to Him—not just at Thanksgiving, but on every day of the year.

Lord, open my eyes to the blessings you've given me. Don't let me take things for granted.

- How does having an ungrateful heart hurt others?
- Why do we praise God?

Only One

Jesus asked, "Were not all ten cleansed?
Where are the other nine?"

LUKE 17:17

Ten very sick men tried frantically to get Jesus' attention as He entered a village on the border of Samaria and Galilee. He was their only hope for an incurable disease. "Jesus, have mercy on us!" they yelled. They stood at a distance—on the outskirts of the city—because by law they weren't allowed to get near to anyone. Due to the horrific effects and contagious nature of their leprosy, they were outcasts from society. Nobody wanted to be near them.

Nobody, that is, except Jesus. His heart was touched by their plight and He said to them, "Go, show yourselves to the priests." (The priests had the ability to call someone clean or unclean.) When the men stepped out in faith, a miracle occurred and they were cleansed of their leprosy.

Here's the stunning thing about this story: only one of the lepers came back to thank Jesus. Only one. Jesus asked, "Where are the other nine?"

He was probably disappointed that nine of them didn't return with thanks. Still, don't we do the exact same thing on many occasions when God blesses us and we just take those things for granted?

Lord, give me a heart of appreciation like the leper who came back to thank you.

- What are some blessings that you've taken for granted?
- How can you be more like the leper who came back to give thanks?

A Spirit of Thankfulness

> But the Lord said to Samuel, "Don't judge by his
> appearance or height, for I have rejected him. The LORD
> doesn't see things the way you see them. People judge
> by outward appearance, but the LORD looks at the heart."
>
> 1 SAMUEL 16:7 NLT

Ted wasn't the least bit grateful for his new shoes. John, on the other hand, was genuinely touched by his gift. These were two young men who had grown up in the same house, so what made the difference? It was their heart attitude.

Ted looked at life with the attitude that blessings were owed to him. He took it all for granted. John's heart was tender. He recognized how hard his dad worked to provide for them.

Now, what about the lepers? Ten of them were healed, but only one came back to thank Jesus. That leper was the one who was most impacted by what had just happened, because not only was his body healed, but his heart was touched as well.

The same is true of us spiritually. If we have the right heart attitude, we have a spirit of thankfulness and appreciation. We see God's blessings as what they are—gifts from a God who loves us so much that He sent us His Son to be sacrificed for our salvation.

Lord, give me a heart that is tender toward you.

- Why did Ted and John react differently to the gift of their shoes?
- What can you do to have a better heart attitude?

Friday

Thanksgiving

Enter into His gates with thanksgiving,
And into His courts with praise.
Be thankful to Him, and bless His name.

PSALM 100:4 NKJV

This week we've discussed the differences in grateful and ungrateful hearts. We've seen that our blessings are gifts from someone who loves us. We've seen the example of the lepers, where only one man came back to thank Jesus. Now it's our turn to put what we've learned into action.

We celebrated Thanksgiving this week. This holiday and its traditions were conceived as a time to thank God for a bountiful harvest. In a broader sense, though, we are grateful for so much more than our food.

Thanksgiving Day should be every day. Let's start that tradition today. What gifts has God given to *you*? Reflect on those things. Grab some paper and a pen, and get specific about it.

Are you healthy? Can you walk? Can you see and hear? Make a list of the physical blessings and specific talents God has given you. Have you ever thanked Him for dying for you? Have you expressed your gratitude for His comfort and strength? Add your spiritual blessings to the list.

Consider your other gifts as well. Thank God for parents who love you, for your clothes, and the other comforts of life. Look around you and expand your list.

Then, make a habit of sharing your lists together as a family.

Lord, thank you for your blessings and for loving me.

- What did you discover from making a list of your blessings?
- How might you help others to see the blessings God has given them?

Annotations

Hearts that are filled with thankfulness and appreciation will overflow into the lives of others—and will touch the heart of God.

. . . .

. . . .

. . . .

. . . .

. . . .

. . . .

. . . .

. . . .

. . . .

. . . .

. . . .

. . . .

. . . .

. . . .

. . . .

. . . .

. . . .

. . . .

. . . .

. . . .

. . . .

. . . .

. . . .

. . . .

. . . .

. . . .

. . . .

Honor

and

Privilege

Week
16

Choosing What's Honorable

For the good that I will to do, I do not do;
but the evil I will not to do, that I practice.

ROMANS 7:19 NKJV

While trying on clothes in the dressing room at the department store, sixteen-year-old Brianna noticed a bulge in one of the pockets. When she slipped her hand in to see what it was, she discovered a gorgeous bracelet.

She started to take it to the sales clerk, but then she stopped. Nobody would know if she took the bracelet. The tags were still on it, so somebody had probably just absentmindedly stuck it in the pocket while trying on the clothes.

She knew it wasn't the honorable thing to do. Her parents had taught her better, but she stood there rationalizing things until she slipped it on and wore it home. Guilt set in that night, especially when her mom noticed the bracelet and she had to lie about where she got it.

She felt horrible, and the sick feeling stayed in her stomach until she finally confessed what she'd done, asked her parents for forgiveness, and took the bracelet back to the store, with a humiliating but heartfelt apology.

Each of us has the privilege of choosing right from wrong. Choosing to do the honorable thing never leaves us with regrets.

Father, when faced with choices, help me to choose what is honorable.

- Why did Brianna feel bad after taking what she wanted?
- Why is it sometimes difficult to make honorable choices?

Unwanted Consequences

Do not be deceived, God is not mocked;
for whatever a man sows, that he will also reap.

GALATIANS 6:7 NKJV

*B*rianna made the wrong decision, and she learned the hard way that there are consequences to our actions. She experienced shame and disgrace because she'd taken something that wasn't hers, lied to her mom about it, and later had to confess her wrongdoing to her parents. One poor choice compounded into several separate transgressions.

The guilt made her sick. Her stomach churned and she had trouble sleeping. She was so ashamed when she had to go back to the store and confess what she'd done, she burst into tears. She was embarrassed because she'd taken something that wasn't hers, and upset that she'd reflected on her parents in a bad manner. All of that angst could have been avoided if she'd made the right decision in the first place—if she'd listened to her conscience.

Here's a tip for you: If you have to struggle to make the decision, if you have to make excuses for why it's the right thing to do, you are probably not making the honorable choice. Making choices is a privilege. We can make wise choices and please God's heart, or we can make unwise ones and end up facing unwanted and uncomfortable consequences.

God, remind me that I will reap what I sow.

- How are consequences attached to our choices?
- What are some ways we can identify poor choices from wise ones?

The Honorable Thing

"A son honors his father,
And a servant his master."

MALACHI 1:6 NKJV

The book of Genesis shares the story of Joseph. We've all heard about his coat of many colors and how he was sold into slavery. Because of his character and work ethic, Joseph rose through the ranks until he became Potiphar's trusted personal servant. God's blessing and privilege was on Joseph, and the blessing was even extended to Potiphar.

Joseph's character was then tested one day when he was placed in a difficult circumstance. Potiphar's wife wanted Joseph to do something that would be wrong, something that would have devastated Potiphar. Joseph refused because he was a man of honor, and because Potiphar had given him such an amazing privilege in his household.

Day after day, Potiphar's wife tried to talk Joseph into doing the immoral thing she desired, but Joseph continued to refuse. Nobody would have known. It would have been a secret between the two of them, but Joseph refused to compromise his principles. He responded with honor because he valued his friendship with Potiphar and his relationship with God.

Even when Potiphar's wife lied about Joseph and got him in serious trouble, Joseph continued to be an honorable man—and he left behind a powerful example for all of us of what it means to do the right thing even when nobody is watching.

Lord, help me to do what's honorable.

- Why did Joseph refuse to do the wrong thing?
- How can we respond to compromising situations with honor?

Thursday

Forewarned Is Forearmed

A person may think their own ways are right,
but the LORD weighs the heart.

PROVERBS 21:2

This week we've learned about the consequences that Brianna faced when she made a dishonorable decision. We've seen how that impacted her physically, emotionally, and spiritually. We've also learned about the story of Joseph and how he purposed in his heart to remain righteous, instead of doing wrong in the eyes of God. He'd built character in his heart *before* he encountered the situation with Potiphar's wife.

That's a valuable lesson for all of us. *Before* we arrive at situations where we might make unwise choices, we need to prepare our hearts so that we'll be ready when we are tested. We need to spend time in God's Word and memorize verses that will be good reminders of how we should live in every circumstance. We need to talk with Him each day so we'll have a close relationship with Him, and we need to ask Him to shine a spotlight on any situation that would grieve His heart.

Character counts, and learning to make wise choices while you're young will equip you for a future in which you will become known as a man or woman of honor.

God, help me to prepare my heart and make wise decisions so I can serve you with honor.

- How should we prepare our hearts before we have to make choices?
- Why is honor important?

Everyday Honor

For I testify that they gave as much as they were able,
and even beyond their ability. Entirely on their own,
they urgently pleaded with us for the privilege of sharing in
this service to the Lord's people. And they exceeded
our expectations: They gave themselves first of all
to the Lord, and then by the will of God also to us.

2 CORINTHIANS 8:3–5

We've talked about privilege and honor this week. Brianna was privileged to shop in the nice store, but lost her honor when she stole the bracelet. Luckily, after her contrition, her honor was restored. Joseph served with integrity and maintained his righteousness even when Potiphar imprisoned him unjustly. God rewarded Joseph for that with a vaulted place of esteem and privilege.

We can honor God by giving our all and doing our best, even in the enticing moments where we might justifiably fail and give in to temptation. Focus on what is good and prepare your heart to resist evil. Look for ways that you can serve Him and others, and don't forget your own family. Having a good attitude about doing chores will honor God. Signing up for a volunteer day at church or going on a mission trip will also allow you to serve Him with honor. Most of all, behave in a praiseworthy way and He will see your heart.

When we honor God in the little things, He will see that He can trust us with the big things as well.

Lord, in all that I do, help me to honor you.

- What are ways we can serve God with honor?
- Why is it important to honor God in the little things?

Annotations

We can avoid shame and disgrace by choosing to live each day with honor—and when we make wise choices, we have nothing to regret.

Compassion
and
Care

Week
17

Please Help Me!

Just as a father has compassion on his children,
So the LORD has compassion on those who fear Him.

PSALM 103:13 NASB

Kirk loved his new skateboard. He'd just worked up the courage to try some tricks that he'd seen at a skateboard exhibition. He was airborne, and everything was going great until some bullies threw sticks where he was supposed to land, and Kirk crashed to the pavement.

He was scraped up and bloody, and it felt as if he'd broken one of his ankles. He tried to sit up, but he was dizzy and in too much pain. The bullies laughed, then grabbed his skateboard and ran away.

Kirk needed help. He waved feebly as a car approached—but the woman went on without stopping. Then he saw a man coming down the sidewalk, but the man crossed to the other side of the street without helping him.

Kirk was too weak to care when the next car came down the street, but this time the car stopped and his dad came running over. "Son, are you okay?" He tenderly cared for the scrapes and cuts, and then he picked Kirk up, put him in the car, and drove him to the hospital.

He had compassion for Kirk—the same kind of compassion that God has for us.

Lord, I'm grateful that you're a God of compassion.

- Why do some people ignore when someone needs compassion?
- How can we become more compassionate and caring?

A Heart That Cares

You must be compassionate,
just as your Father is compassionate.

Luke 6:36 NLT

*Y*esterday we saw several different reactions to Kirk's plight. The bullies enjoyed knowing that they'd caused pain to another human being. The woman in the first car didn't pull over; her initial instinct was to stop and help the young man, but she hardened her heart to the sight in front of her. Her schedule was jammed that day, and if she stopped, she'd be late for work and might even get blood on her new outfit. The elderly man who walked down the sidewalk just didn't want to be bothered. Fearful of getting involved, he was indifferent to the pain of the young man lying injured on the sidewalk.

The difference came when Kirk's father arrived on the scene and saw his injured son. He loved his boy, and he had deep compassion for whatever concerned his son. That's such a beautiful picture of how God sees us. If something concerns us, it concerns Him. He comes to our aid immediately, with tender love and compassion. He wants us to have that same compassion when we see others who are hurting or in need.

Lord, help me to be more concerned for others than I am about myself. Give me a heart of compassion.

- Why does God want us to have compassion for others?
- Why are we sometimes more concerned about ourselves than others?

Wednesday

The Man on the Street

He answered, "'Love the Lord your God with all your heart
and with all your soul and with all your strength and with
all your mind'; and, 'Love your neighbor as yourself.'"

LUKE 10:27

Jesus says, "Love your neighbor as yourself." Give some serious
thought to what that involves and implies. In Luke 10, He
shares a parable that sheds more light on it.

A man was journeying from Jerusalem to Jericho when he was
viciously attacked and robbed. The bandits beat him so badly
that he was half dead when they left him lying on the road. They
even took his clothes.

A priest walked by—someone who should have had compassion on the man—but he crossed to the other side of the road and
kept going. One of the Levites saw the wounded man, but he also
crossed to the other side of the road and avoided any interaction.

However, when a Samaritan traveled by, he saw the injured
man and had compassion on him. He stopped and bandaged his
wounds, then took him to an inn and cared for him. When the
Samaritan man had to leave, he even paid the innkeeper to care
for the man.

Can you imagine what that kindness meant to the man who'd
been beaten and robbed?

**Lord, give me a heart of compassion when I see others in
need.**

- Why did the Samaritan stop to help the man when
  others didn't?
- What is Jesus illustrating with this parable?

Boomerang

"A new commandment I give to you,
that you love one another; as I have loved you,
that you also love one another."

JOHN 13:34 NKJV

Think about what the world might be like without compassionate people. There wouldn't be doctors or nurses to make you feel better. If your house caught on fire, it would just burn to the ground because firefighters wouldn't have cared enough to extinguish the blaze. The police wouldn't be there if you had a problem, and your pastor wouldn't show up to comfort you when you buried a loved one. Your parents wouldn't even cook your dinner or wash your clothes because they lacked any consideration for your welfare.

Thank goodness we don't live in a world like that! Jesus encourages us to be more compassionate and loving, but the world encourages us to be selfish and self-absorbed. He is a God of love, one whose heart is touched by whatever concerns us. The closer we come to know Him, the more like Him we become, and the more others will see Him in us.

Acting considerately and affectionately toward others has a boomerang effect. It often ends up blessing us even more than those to whom we've extended kindness, and sometimes it's through those deeds that hearts are reached for God in ways they wouldn't have been otherwise.

Lord, help me to love like you do.

- What are some instances where you have received compassion?
- How does being compassionate affect you personally?

A Life of Compassion

If anyone has material possessions and sees a brother
or sister in need but has no pity on them,
how can the love of God be in that person?

1 JOHN 3:17

There are numerous Bible stories about people who were compassionate and caring. After her husband's death, Ruth could have gone back to her country, but out of love, she chose to go with her grieving mother-in-law. Four friends cared so deeply for their paralytic friend they dislodged a roof and lowered him through, just so he could see Jesus? He was healed through their faith. Jesus shows us that faith and compassion have healing properties. There's no finer example of compassion than the life of Christ.

Contemplate what the story of your life will tell about how compassionate and caring you were? It's wonderful to hear stories about awesome instances of compassion, but sometimes the most remarkable and inspiring tales come from the little moments. The time you bought a hot meal and took it to the homeless man on the corner. The instance where you didn't buy a new outfit so your sister could have one. The day you cleaned out the garage so your dad wouldn't have to.

Those might seem like little things to you, but they meant something special to the recipients—and to the heart of God.

Lord, open my eyes to the needs around me.

- What can you do to show compassion this week?
- How do you feel after you've done something nice for someone?

Annotations

Compassion affects both the person who receives it and the person who gives it. It pleases the heart of God when we care for others.

....
....
....
....
....
....
....
....
....
....
....
....
....
....
....
....
....
....
....
....
....
....
....
....
....
....

Hospitality and Generosity

Week 18

Almost Everyone

Offer hospitality to one another without grumbling.

1 PETER 4:9

*A*bigail was excited. Her mom had just said she could have a Christmas party and invite all her friends. She had a fun afternoon planning the menu, looking online for decoration ideas, and making the guest list.

That night after dinner, Abigail pulled the lists out and said, "Mom, look at all the great ideas I came up with this afternoon."

Her mom looked over the menu and declared that everything sounded delicious. She also loved all the ideas for the table and room decorations, but when she got to the guest list and read through the names, she got an odd look on her face. "You have every name from our co-op group on the list except Brendan, and all the kids your age in our neighborhood except Mary. Why didn't you invite them to your party?"

"Well ... Brendan doesn't really fit in with everybody else, and Mary is so quiet she hardly ever says anything."

Her mom replied, "All I'm going to say is that I want you to pray about it and think how you'd feel if you were the only one in the group not invited."

Two days later when the invitations went out, God had touched Abigail's heart so that she was generous enough to extend hospitality to everyone.

Lord, give me a generous and loving spirit.

- Why was it a poor choice for Abigail to exclude those two friends?
- How can we extend hospitality to others?

The Benefits of Kindness

Be kind and compassionate to one another.

Ephesians 4:32

We learned how Abigail almost made a mistake and hurt some people. After praying and listening to her mom and to God, she quit being stingy with her hospitality and invited Mary and Brendan to her Christmas party.

Have you ever been the one who was excluded from a party or other event? That's hard and it's hurtful, but if we're wise, we'll learn from those experiences and make sure that *we* don't make other people sad by doing the same thing.

Abigail learned another valuable lesson from this experience, because after Brendan came to her Christmas party, she realized that he'd been shy and lonely, and once he got to know everyone better, he was a lot of fun. She also discovered that one of the reasons that Mary was so quiet was because her mom had cancer and was undergoing chemotherapy. Abigail's party brought some joy into her life at a time when she needed it.

Sometimes when we look beyond the surface, we can find an unexpected bond with people. By doing what was right, Abigail showed kindness and encouraged the hearts of two people who needed to know that somebody cared about them. She was grateful knowing she had narrowly avoided inadvertently hurt anyone.

Lord, help me to extend kindness and to be hospitable to everyone.

- Why are we encouraged to practice hospitality?
- How is hospitality the opposite of loneliness?

The Ultimate Generosity

*"For God so loved the world that He gave
His only begotten Son, that whoever believes in Him
should not perish but have everlasting life."*

JOHN 3:16 NKJV

A holy hush filled the stable as Jesus was born. A moment that seemed so simple, yet it was anything but that. This was the day salvation was born. Mary and Joseph had waited a long time for that moment, but they certainly hadn't expected the birth to happen in a stable filled with animals. They'd planned something far better—but God had known that the simple surroundings were appropriate and that they signified that His gift was available to all, no matter whether they were rich or not.

Nobody does hospitality better than God. He includes everyone in His invitation to accept Jesus as their Savior. As well, nobody does generosity better than God. He gave what was most precious to Him—His Son. That's the ultimate generosity. That babe in the manger was love wrapped in swaddling clothes, a priceless gift that's available to all of us.

At Christmas, we give gifts to our family and friends, but the best gift we can ever give is the one that was given to us on that first Christmas Day: Jesus!

God, thank you for the generous gift of your Son.

- How does the gift of Jesus fit with our theme of generosity?
- How does hospitality tie in with the birth of Jesus?

Thursday

A Most Precious Gift

For by grace you have been saved through faith, and that
not of yourselves; it is the gift of God.

EPHESIANS 2:8–9 NKJV

We celebrate Christmas this week. It's a special time of year
filled with festive decorations, brightly wrapped gifts, culinary treats, and fun times with loved ones, but the main reason
we celebrate is because of the birth of Jesus.

Jesus lived a life of generosity, giving freely of Himself. Even
when He was tired, He healed people. He spoke to the ones society shunned, the lepers and the sinners. He gave us a perfect
picture of hospitality.

Many of us are stingy when it comes to sharing or giving away
something that we love. What if God had been selfish with His
Son?

Most of us have friends and family members who are dear
to us. If they need something and we have it, we are generous
enough to give it to them, but we are unwilling to give up *somebody* who is precious to us. It's a typical human trait.

God gave up what was *most* precious to Him: His beloved
Son. He did that for us. Because of that, we don't even have to
contemplate a future without Him in our lives.

Lord, thank you for your sacrifice—your amazing
generosity—and for the priceless gift of Jesus.

- How would our lives be different if God had been selfish with His Son?
- Why was God's gift of His Son such an amazing sacrifice?

A Season of Giving

"Every man shall give as he is able, according to the
blessing of the LORD your God which He has given you."

DEUTERONOMY 16:17 NKJV

Sometimes Christmas can be an all-about-me time as we think about what we want for Christmas gifts. There's nothing wrong with receiving gifts, but we should consider Christmas as a season of giving. Let's think today about some specific ways we can be generous and hospitable throughout Christmas.

We can give the gift of our time. Christmas is often extra busy. Help your parents prepare the food for Christmas dinner or offer to wrap the gifts for them (not yours!) Your church probably needs volunteers to help with the Christmas play or to deliver potted plants or treat bags to your elderly members. Those individual members could likely use your helpfulness, as well, in their holiday preparations.

Maybe you can earn some extra money and buy gifts for children who otherwise wouldn't get something for Christmas, or help a missionary by sending some of those gifts to an orphanage abroad.

We can give from our hearts. It's a gift to tell people what they mean to us. Write a letter or a card to your parents, your grandparents, your siblings, or a close friend. Share why they're special to you. They will treasure it.

Father, open my eyes to ways I can bless others.

- What are some ways you can give to others?
- How does it make you feel when you give to someone else?

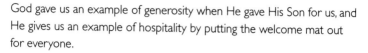

Annotations

God gave us an example of generosity when He gave His Son for us, and He gives us an example of hospitality by putting the welcome mat out for everyone.

....
....
....
....
....
....
....
....
....
....
....
....
....
....
....
....
....
....
....
....
....
....
....
....
....

Three-Week Break

Decisiveness and Resolve

Week
19

A Firm Resolve

But you, dear friends, by building yourselves up
in your most holy faith and praying in the Holy Spirit,
keep yourselves in God's love as you wait for the mercy of
our Lord Jesus Christ to bring you to eternal life.

JUDE 20–21

*B*rian's pastor often preached about the importance of reading God's Word, and he suggested setting a goal to read the Bible through in a year. Brian thought that was a great idea. He'd even started it a couple of times in years past, but he'd quit after a week or so.

He was more mature now, though, and as New Year's Day approached, he resolved that *this* year he was going to read his Bible through from cover to cover. Some days, when he was tired or extra busy, he struggled to keep his promise, but he had made a schedule and was determined to keep it.

The benefits were awesome. He learned new things and drew closer to God, and his attitude was better because he was trying to be like Jesus. By the time he was eighteen, he'd read his Bible through six times, and as a result of his commitment, he was so changed that others noticed the difference in him.

Lord, give me a resolve to read your Word.

- Brian had failed before in his decision to read the Bible through in a year. What made the difference this time?
- How did reading his Bible change Brian's life?

Tuesday

Reaching the Goal

I can do all things through Christ who strengthens me.

PHILIPPIANS 4:13 NKJV

*B*rian learned that setting a goal is an important part of any decision. His decisiveness—backed by prayers for God to help him—made a big difference. If he'd been hesitant in his goal, he likely wouldn't have achieved it. Missing even just one day might have derailed him from his efforts. Even so, he didn't waver, and because of that resolve, he became a young man of principle.

There's no way we can read God's Word without it changing us for the better. When people started noticing the change in Brian, something awesome happened. Conversations at the dinner table often focused on things in the Bible that Brian had just discovered. Some of his friends were inspired by what he was doing, and they began reading their Bibles.

When he proved to God that he was going to be faithful, God began opening doors for Brian. His pastor was touched by his commitment, and he helped raise the money for Brian's trip to the Holy Land so he could see the Bible come to life. He also asked Brian to teach a Sunday school class for the younger children at church. Brian's resolve to faithfully read God's Word changed his life.

Lord, help me to be faithful.

- Why is it important to set goals?
- What led to God opening doors of opportunity for Brian?

Taming the Lions

Three times a day he got down on his knees and prayed,
giving thanks to his God, just as he had done before.

DANIEL 6:10

*D*aniel was a decisive man of principle. When he was a young man, he resolved that he wouldn't defile himself with the royal food. God honored that, helping him to excel so much that King Darius considered putting him in charge of the whole realm. Daniel's excellence was a direct result of his disciplined spiritual life.

Some men were jealous of Daniel's success, and they searched for anything they could use against him, but he lived such a pure life that nobody could find fault with him. They plotted, instead, to attack his faith. They talked the king into announcing a decree that, for a period of thirty days, anybody found praying to anyone but King Darius would be thrown into a pit of lions.

The elderly Daniel learned about the edict, but his resolve didn't falter; he still knelt in front of his window and prayed to God three times a day. The king was sorrowful to sentence Daniel to a certain death in the lions' pit, but what the evil men had meant for harm, God used for His glory. God sealed the lions' mouths shut and they didn't touch Daniel. A relieved King Darius shared that impassioned testimony throughout his kingdom.

Lord, help me to serve you faithfully.

- Why didn't Daniel modify the way he chose to pray?
- Why didn't the lions harm Daniel?

A Deep Resolve

"I decree that everyone throughout my kingdom should
tremble with fear before the God of Daniel. For he is the
living God, and he will endure forever. His kingdom will
never be destroyed, and his rule will never end.
He rescues and saves his people; he performs miraculous
signs and wonders in the heavens and on earth. He has
rescued Daniel from the power of the lions."

DANIEL 6:26–27 NLT

We've seen how Daniel's and Brian's resolve impacted their lives. In Daniel's case, God kept him safe in a den of hungry lions. He didn't have a scratch on him. Not even one!

News of that event spread throughout the kingdom. The actions of the Almighty on behalf of His faithful, diligent servant bore witness to His great power, for *all* to see. A grateful King Darius left nothing to rumor or speculation, however, and issued a proclamation to his subjects declaring that Daniel's God was the living God, one who could deliver and rescue His people. For Daniel, too, escaping unscathed and seeing the tremendous transformation in his monarch must have blessed him. His decision as a young man to live for God equipped him for the moment when his faith would be tested.

Consider how Daniel's faithfulness brought glory to God. Others notice when we serve God—or when we don't. In this instance, one man's resolve impacted an entire nation.

Lord, give me a resolve like Daniel had. Give me a testimony of faithfulness.

- How do you think this experience affected Daniel?
- How do our actions spiritually affect others?

Resolve in Action

"You shall walk after the LORD your God and fear Him,
and keep His commandments and obey His voice;
you shall serve Him and hold fast to Him."

DEUTERONOMY 13:4 NKJV

We've discussed the impact of Daniel's resolve. How did Brian's resolve to serve God impact his life?

When he was a teenager, other teens sometimes made fun of Brian for carrying his Bible around and reading it. Their words were hurtful, but they couldn't break Brian's resolute determination. He is thirty-two years old now, married with two children, and now the seeds sown by young Brian's faithful testimony as a teenager are bearing fruit.

Moms of the guys who'd made fun of him come to Brian to plead, "My son isn't close to God. He always told me that you were the real deal and he respected you. Would you talk to him?" People repeatedly reach out for his leadership and input. He'd had no idea that he had impacted others in such a way.

Now he's a youth pastor, reaching countless lives, but none of that would have happened if he hadn't resolved as a young man that He was going to read God's Word and live for Him.

New Year's Day is a time to make resolutions, and the best two you will ever make is that you'll read your Bible faithfully and that you'll live for God. It's not too late!

Lord, I resolve today that I'm going to live for you.

- Why does it take resolve to live for God?
- How does our culture today discourage faith in God?

Annotations

Resolve requires a decisive moment. Deep faith in God also doesn't occur spontaneously; it starts with a resolve to learn about God and then serve Him.

Resourcefulness and Initiative

Week 20

Be the Leader

"So in everything, do to others what you would have them
do to you, for this sums up the Law and the Prophets."

MATTHEW 7:12

When Neil arrived at basketball practice, a new boy was on the court, dribbling by himself. He was short and skinny. The boys on the team whispered among themselves and snickered. One even pointed a finger at the boy.

"Hey, Neil, look at the new boy. I bet you don't want him on your team."

Neil looked at over at the new kid. He didn't really want to go out on a limb, but he remembered the time his family had moved to a new town and how alone he felt. As his friends watched, Neil walked over and put out his hand. "Hi! I'm Neil."

"I'm Tyler." The boy smiled.

"Guys, I think Tyler would make a great guard. C'mon, Tyler, let's shoot some hoops."

The rest of the team soon followed. Neil's leadership effectively changed the whole mood of their practice.

The Bible is clear about who is to take the initiative, or the first step, in relationships and actions with others. We are to act toward others the way we would have them act to us. This is also known as the Golden Rule. Jesus taught this principle in His Sermon on the Mount, and it is still pertinent today. For believers, it is the greatest advice for living in harmony with others.

Lord, help me to always treat others as I would like to be treated.

- How can you take the initiative with your friends?
- How do you feel when others make fun of you?

You Can Do It!

"By what authority are you doing these things,
and who gave you this authority?"

MATTHEW 21:23 ESV

"Try another way," Mom said.

"But, Mom, it's not easy. I can't figure out how to create this visual of DNA."

"If it's easy, it's hardly worth doing. Use your initiative and be resourceful. You'll get it."

"Mom, you know I can't make a square out of match sticks. And look at Shera. It took her five minutes to make a plan and then build her model."

"You aren't competing with your sister. I know you can do it. Don't put pressure on yourself. Think it through and pray about a solution."

Often we find ourselves in a hard situation; we just can't see a way out. When initiative and resourcefulness are needed, we can count on God to provide that for us if we will rely on Him. He is the God of creativity and resourcefulness.

As you go about your day, ask Him to show you new ways to do things. If you encounter a challenge, step up and meet it head on, knowing that the God that created the platypus will overcome your lack of imagination with His limitless resourcefulness and creativity.

Lord, help me meet every challenge with your resourcefulness.

- The last time you thought you couldn't do something, did you pray and ask God to equip you for the task?
- How did He respond?

Be an Encourager

For Titus not only welcomed our appeal, but he is coming
to you with much enthusiasm and on his own initiative.

<small>2 Corinthians 8:17</small>

In 2 Corinthians 8, Paul writes a letter to the church concerning their giving. His encouragement to complete their task of giving with a willing attitude spurs them all. Paul obviously wanted them to succeed.

Paul's coworker, Titus, also wanted to see the church complete their task of giving. He stepped up to visit the church and be another cheerleader for them, and he did it on his own initiative. In other words, Paul didn't assign Titus this duty. Titus realized he could be of help and generously volunteered to serve.

You could do the same thing Titus did for the church. Have you ever felt God speaking to your heart and prompting you to go somewhere or to do something? Maybe He wanted you to go to a friend and offer encouragement concerning something he or she was learning or working on.

When you hear that small voice in your heart, listen and act. You will bless someone else and will likely receive an even greater blessing yourself.

Lord, show me how I can take the initiative and bless others.

- Who in your life needs encouragement? Commit to contacting at least one person this week.
- Think of a time when you heard God's voice and acted. What did you learn from that?

Thursday

Friends

He stores up sound wisdom for the upright;
he is a shield to those who walk in integrity,
guarding the paths of justice
and watching over the way of his saints.

PROVERBS 2:7–8 ESV

Marc and Joey had been best friends and next-door neighbors for as long as they could remember.

Whenever they wanted to meet in the clubhouse by the creek, Marc put his sweatshirt over the blinds in his room. If Joey left his sweatshirt over the back-porch rail, that was his signal. The boys had to be inventive to find a way to let each other know when to meet because they didn't have cell phones.

They were resourceful while building their clubhouse as well. They asked for scraps of wood from construction sites, and left-over paint as well.

Spending time with good friends is fun, and many times you need to take the initiative to make time in your busy schedule for them.

Jesus is the only friend with whom we don't have to schedule time. He is always there. Just start talking to Him and He will listen. He is your best friend and will provide you with wisdom and sound counsel in every situation.

Lord, show me the resources to reach people for you.

- Name one thing you and your best friend like to do together. Why do you enjoy that activity?
- Share about a time when you and a friend took the initiative to be kind to someone.

Stepping Out

"Israel's leaders took charge, and the people gladly followed.
Praise the LORD!"

JUDGES 5:2 NLT

This chapter of Judges is known as Deborah's song. Deborah begins with praise to God, and the leaders of Israel step out and others gladly follow. Even in wartime a long time ago, when leaders took the initiative to step out, others followed. We often think of leaders taking the initiative in times of conflict and war, both in times past and today, but there are many other life situations where the same principles apply.

We have talked about initiative this week. Sometimes it takes courage to take the initiative because that means taking the lead, if only for a moment. Reflect on why you might feel compelled to act. That might be God's plan. We have also discussed resourcefulness. That can also mean "thinking outside the box" or showing initiative. It may seem risky, but with risk can come great rewards.

Seek God's guidance in these moments of uncertainty. He will show you how to proceed if you will just let Him and trust in His guidance. In fact, God showed initiative by reaching out to you first. He loves you—and all of us—so much that He showed us how to love others by sending His Son, Jesus, to sacrifice His life for us: the ultimate example of love!

Lord, thank you for showing me ways I can take the initiative and bless others.

- This week, what are two ways you can show initiative that will benefit others?
- How do you feel when you know God is asking you to take the initiative and be resourceful?

Annotations

Taking initiative and being resourceful are two ways we can use the creativity God has given us. Find a way to use it today that will bring glory to Him.

....

....

....

....

....

....

....

....

....

....

....

....

....

....

....

....

....

....

....

....

....

....

....

....

....

Truthfulness
and
Candor

Week
21

Straight from the Heart

"And you shall know the truth,
and the truth shall make you free."

JOHN 8:32 NKJV

*M*adison had avoided eye contact with her mom since they'd started school. Finally, she said, "Mom, can I talk with you?"

Moments later, the two gathered in the family room. Madison looked at the floor as she said, "I need to tell you something. Remember last week when Brenda and I went to the mall for our friend-day-out shopping trip? Well, while she was trying on clothes in the dressing room, I sat on a bench outside the store. Some girls I know came by and said, 'Did we see you talking to Brenda? She's so frumpy.'"

Her mom asked what she'd replied.

Shame colored Madison's face. "I told them I barely knew her." She then shared how they'd asked why she was even talking to Brenda, and she had replied, "I feel sorry for her since she's so uncool." Tears dripped to the floor as Madison choked out, "I've felt awful ever since then. I've asked God to forgive me, but knowing that I was both untruthful and unkind is eating me alive."

Madison felt somewhat better after telling her mom the truth, but the knowledge that she had been untruthful about a dear friend left lasting pain in her heart.

Lord, help me to be truthful, even when it isn't easy.

- How did Madison's lack of truthfulness affect her?
- What would have been a better response to the questioning girls?

An Honest Friend

An honest witness tells the truth,
but a false witness tells lies.

PROVERBS 12:17

*M*adison's mom knew that this was the time for candor—open honesty—with her daughter. They talked about how Madison had lied about her friend, Brenda.

Her mom asked, "Why weren't you truthful when the girls asked you those questions?"

"I didn't want them to think I was like her, because I know they don't like her."

"Why was it so important for them to like you?"

"Well, they always look so put together, with perfect hair and makeup."

"Being stylish is fine, but while those girls may be pretty on the outside, are they as lovely on the inside?"

"They're pretty mean, actually," Madison said. "They make fun of people all the time."

"So what have you learned from this experience, Madison?"

"I've learned that I was looking for the wrong kind of friends—when I already had an amazing one. I learned that I should have been more loyal to Brenda. I learned that telling the truth is always better than being dishonest. And that it makes me feel awful when I tell a lie."

Lord, thank you for parents who tell the truth.

- How does it help us to have people who will speak to us with candor?
- What lessons did Madison's mom help her learn?

The Denial

Jesus said to him, "Assuredly, I say to you that this night,
before the rooster crows, you will deny Me three times."

MATTHEW 26:34 NKJV

*J*esus had a personal impact on Simon Peter's life. Peter had walked with Him, seen His mighty acts, and witnessed His compassion—so you'd think that Peter would be his staunchest defender, especially when the crucifixion of Jesus was mere days away. He assured Jesus that he would stand by Him even when others didn't. Jesus replied that before the rooster crowed the next morning, Peter would deny Him three times. Peter was terribly upset by that comment, declaring he'd die before that happened.

When Jesus was arrested at Gethsemane and led away to Caiaphas the high priest, Peter followed and sat in the courtyard. A servant girl asserted that Peter had been with Jesus, but Peter responded that he didn't know what she was talking about.

When he went and sat by the gate, another woman remarked that Peter had been with Jesus of Galilee, and he answered that he didn't even know the man. A man then told Peter that his way of speaking was like that of Jesus, and Peter cursed and swore and claimed that he didn't know Jesus.

Later, Peter's lack of truthfulness broke his heart.

Lord, help me to never deny that I know you.

- Why do you think Peter lied about knowing Jesus?
- How did Peter's lack of truthfulness impact him?

Acceptable Words

Let the words of my mouth and the meditation of my heart
Be acceptable in Your sight,
O Lord, my strength and my Redeemer.

PSALM 19:14 NKJV

*W*e make decisions based on a variety of things. Madison was untruthful because she wanted the trendy and popular girls to like her. Because of that, she betrayed someone who'd been her dear friend for many years.

Peter lied out of fear and shame. He betrayed the God who loved him enough to give His life for him. Can you imagine how that grieved the heart of Jesus? Both Madison and Peter learned there are consequences when we aren't truthful.

Madison's mom loved her enough to respond to her situation with candor. Through His Word, God does the same. Loyalty to God and to others is a valuable trait. Hurting those we love is never a good thing, and grieving the heart of God should be avoided at all costs.

As our verse today says, let's make the words that come out of our mouths acceptable in God's eyes. Since the words that we speak come from our hearts, the values we hold in our hearts are an important starting point.

Father, let my words—and my heart—be pleasing to you. Help me to be a faithful servant to you, and a loyal, honest, and kind friend.

- Why might we make decisions to be untruthful?
- How are our hearts and truthfulness tied together?

Truth with Love

Little children, let us not love in word or talk
but in deed and in truth.

JOHN 3:18 ESV

It turned out that Brenda had overheard Madison's comments. This weighed heavily on Brenda and Madison's relationship until Brenda took the initiative and broached the conversation with Madison.

"You heard that?" Madison asked, mortified.

Brenda nodded.

Madison, quickly blurted out, "I'm so sorry. They made me feel bad about myself, and I behaved poorly. I've realized how precious our friendship is, and I won't put it in jeopardy again."

Brenda smiled. "I know. It's hard with people like that, so I get it. And I know you are my very best friend. I'm just glad you realized it too."

Madison was grateful she had such a wise, truthful friend.

It helps when we have someone who will speak the truth to us with grace. Candor means that we share with open honesty, but that should be tempered with kindness and love. Never speak in haste or when you're angry. Think and pray about what you'll say before you say it. Ask God to give you the right words to say— and the right motives.

Learning to become a person of candor when we're young will impact us for the rest of our lives, and God loves it when He sees us becoming men and women with truthful hearts.

Father, help me to speak the truth with love.

- How can you become more truthful?
- What should you do when you respond to others with candor?

Annotations

Having someone who will speak to you with candor is a gift. When you tell the truth on a consistent basis, others, including God, will see you as trustworthy.

....
....
....
....
....
....
....
....
....
....
....
....
....
....
....
....
....
....
....
....
....
....
....
....

Orderliness
and
Management

Week
22

Restore Order

Let all things be done decently and in order.

1 Corinthians 14:40 nkjv

*M*om stood at the door of Virginia's room. "Honey, I can hardly walk in here. How can you find anything in all of this chaos?"

"Oh, Mom, I know exactly where everything is."

"That may be, but it could be dangerous if you had to get up in the middle of the night."

"Mom, I'm just not like you. You want everything in a certain place. I walk into your bedroom and it feels almost clinical. No mess anywhere. It's ridiculous."

"It's not ridiculous. A disorganized mess is a distraction. No wonder you struggle to finish your homework. Look at that cluttered desk! And remember when you couldn't find your other shoe before church last Sunday?"

"But Mom ..."

"No buts. God created the order of the universe, and there must be a good reason for that, right?"

"Okay. I'll work on it as soon as I finish my homework."

God wants us to live orderly lives, and the best place to start is at home. Organization can then overflow into all other parts of our lives, making us more efficient and productive. It can also bring order to your relationship with God. Knowing the many ways God loves you makes it easier to share with others.

Lord, help me to live an orderly life so I bring honor to you.

- ° How can you address one area of your life that needs order?
- ° How can you introduce order into your spiritual life?

Let's Get Out!

For God is not a God of disorder but of peace.

1 CORINTHIANS 14:33

"*P*eople!" the announcer shouted. "We've got to evacuate the stadium! It's dangerous to remain. Please exit as fast as you can!" Chaos ensued as all five thousand people headed for the exits. There was no plan, just massive panic as everyone tried to get out. People pushed and shoved as they jockeyed for a path. Some even fell down. Children cried and screamed.

Moments later, a more measured voice issued a more orderly plan. "Ladies and gentlemen, you're attention, please. There's been an emergency, and we need for everyone in the east section of the stadium to exit through the nearest door to your right. The west section, use the doors to the left, please. There is no need for alarm, and there is plenty of time to get out safely. Don't push or shove, but keep moving."

God is the God of order and good management in every situation. In fact, it is primarily though the order God created in Genesis that we experience God.

Many situations can be approached in different ways, as illustrated above. If you are in a situation that feels confusing and chaotic, stop and ask God to help you make order of it. Better yet, start every day by asking God to help sort everything that might be confusing.

Lord, replace chaos with order in my life.

- How could your spiritual life become less chaotic?
- Why does God not desire chaos for your life?

Consequences of Dishonest Management

"So he called him in and asked him, 'What is this
I hear about you? Give an account of your management,
because you cannot be manager any longer.'"

LUKE 16:2

*J*esus told the story about the manager of a rich man's affairs. All seemed well until the rich man requested an audit of the books. The manager was fired, but not before a visit to his master's debtors. To make it better for himself and to gain their favor, the manager forgave part of their debt.

The master praised his manager for his cleverness despite his dishonesty. The man lost his job because his managerial style was neither orderly nor honest. He made choices that cost him his livelihood. Being an effective manager stems from a love of people and a heart that wants to do the right thing.

We all face management decisions each day. For instance, if you just put all the ingredients for a cake in the oven thinking you'll mix them together after baking, nobody will get any cake after dinner. A recipe is like a checklist, which must be completed in order.

Life is like cooking. It requires an ordered plan and God has all the recipes. He has perfect order. Pray for God's guidance in making the choices you face daily.

Lord, help me to always make decisions that honor you.

° How can you order your plans for your future?
° When have you witnessed poor time management?

A Lesson from the Ants

Go to the ant, you sluggard;
consider its ways and be wise!

Proverbs 6:6

Have you ever stood and watched a colony of ants at work? They travel in straight lines as they carry food into their anthills. Rarely do you see an ant stray. Imagine the chaos if every ant decided to go its own way, especially as it is estimated that there are about one million ants for every person in the world? The number of ants in a colony, each doing his own disorderly thing—that would be total confusion.

As Proverbs indicates, we can learn several things from the ants: the value of hard work, how to labor with others, how order eliminates chaos, how even large groups can work hard together, and that even though you may be small, you are important to the cause of your family.

Ants work together to bring food for the survival of the colony. Other ants serve other purposes. Though ants may have less diverse roles than humans, their powerful example should not be lost on us.

God put each of us where He wanted us. You are not in your family by mistake, and everyone operates better when all the family members fulfill their respective positions and roles. When you know where you belong, you can be assured that God will equip you to fill your spot well.

Lord, thank you for my place in the family. Help me to fill it well.

- What do you see as your place in the family order?
- What happens if you don't practice order in your life or if you mismanage your time?

Be Ready

Do your best to present yourself to God as one approved,
a worker who does not need to be ashamed
and who correctly handles the word of truth.

2 Timothy 2:15

*H*ow does one become approved by God? There are lots of things on this checklist, with the most important one being to love Him with all your heart, soul, and mind. That garners His immediate appreciation. Think about other things that please Him greatly: loving others, studying His Word, spending time with Him, worshipping Him, and sharing your faith with others.

Now think about the orderly approach to sharing your faith. How would you manage that Great Commission? As believers, we should be ready to tell about Him at all times.

What would you put on your checklist to prepare you to serve God in spreading His Word? Knowing God's Word, preparing a few sentences of your testimony, and praying for God to use you will keep you ready to share a few words about Him with others. You needn't be nervous about sharing your faith if you do so with honesty and sincerity. Let them see the reason for the joy you have.

Lord, keep me always ready to be your spokesperson.

- What happened the first time you shared about your faith to a nonbeliever?
- What one area of your spiritual life can you manage better?

Annotations

Orderliness eliminates chaos and confusion. Good management creates a smooth-running environment. Do your best to incorporate both into your life.

Flexibility
and
Grace

Week
23

Accepting Change

Now faith is the assurance of things hoped for,
the conviction of things not seen.

HEBREWS 11:1 ESV

A tear trickled down Charlotte's cheek. "But, Mom, you said I could go to the party. I've been planning this with my friends for weeks."

"I know, honey. But I had no idea Grandma and Grandpa would decide to meet us halfway from New York for the weekend. We only see them a couple of times a year. And it's Grandpa's birthday."

"But I promised my friends I'd come. How am I going to explain this to them?"

"I know you're disappointed, but your grandparents really want to see all of you grandchildren."

"I'm not going to like this trip," Charlotte warned.

"Sometimes things beyond our control change our plans, but we must learn how to cope, with a generous attitude."

Charlotte knew Mom was right. "All right. I'm sorry. Maybe I can make it up to my friends next week instead."

Mom smiled. "That's my girl. I love your grace-filled attitude."

Being flexible, or adaptable, makes challenges go a lot easier. Life doesn't always follow the plan that we create, but God is pleased when we remain flexible with our schedules and plans, because His plans are always best for us.

Lord, bless my life with flexibility, especially when you are the one who makes the change.

- How do you react when you experience disappointment, as Charlotte did?
- Why does it please God when you are flexible?

Don't Wait

For I, the LORD your God, hold your right hand; it is I
who say to you, "Fear not, I am the one who helps you."

ISAIAH 41:13 ESV

*G*raham laughed. He had a four-year-old on one arm, a little boy riding piggyback, and another child clinging to his waist. *Why did I wait so long to come on this mission trip?*

His church had sponsored the youth mission trip for years, but he loved his job as a lifeguard, and if he left for a week, he wouldn't get paid. Friends begged him to go, youth workers encouraged him, and he even felt as if God would want him to go. And yet, Graham had resisted, reasoning that surely God preferred him to save for his education.

However, this year Graham had given in and signed up for the trip. The week was life changing for him. Spending time teaching children in another part of the world was amazing. He learned to gracefully incorporate new experiences into his firm desires for college.

When he got home, Graham told his mom, "The best thing I learned is that when God tells you to do something, you should do it the first time. Don't resist."

Lord, may I always follow your leading.

- Has there ever been a time when you felt God wanted you to do something but you resisted? What was the resolution?
- How can we best discern God's direction for us?

Granted Grace

"But in your great mercy you did not put an end to them or
abandon them, for you are a gracious and merciful God."

NEHEMIAH 9:31

*H*annah looked at her watch. She was late, and she knew
her mom and dad were strict about curfew. Pushing a little
harder on the gas pedal, she thought, *I've got to make it home on
time.*

"Uh-oh." In her rearview mirror she saw flashing blue lights.
She pulled over into a gas station.

"Miss, you seem to be in a hurry," the police officer said.

"Yes, sir. I guess I am. I'm sorry." Tears pooled in Hannah's
eyes. "I'm really sorry."

The officer checked Hannah's license and registration. "I'm
going to let you off with a warning, young lady. But from now on,
pay attention to the speed limit. I want you to arrive safely."

"Thank you. I will."

The officer returned to his car, and Hannah could think of
only one thing: grace. The officer used flexibility in dispensing
justice for her infraction. *I deserved that ticket. And because of
grace, I didn't get it.*

As she pulled into her driveway, Hannah realized that God
often accorded her grace. She vowed to do her best to be deserving of that.

**Lord, thank you for your grace, and for giving it even though
I don't deserve it.**

- What is your definition of grace?
- You are God's messenger of grace. Name one person you
  need to extend grace to today.

Abram's Example

The Lord is good to all;
he has compassion on all he has made.

PSALM 145:9

*A*bram and his family were living in Haran when God told him to take his family and move. They had their roots down there. They had livestock and land, friends and family, so just imagine what it must have felt like when God instructed them to pack up their belongings and move to a new location. To move meant storing up food for the months of journey, loading their household things onto beasts of burden, and organizing everything for a lengthy walk.

Abram could have answered God, "That's not going to work for me. I have too much to do." He could have reasonably argued that he needed to stay and take care of his father. But he didn't.

Instead, Abram listened to God and was prepared to follow His leading at any moment, to go anywhere. Abram, at seventy-five years old, certainly exhibited great flexibility.

You show you are flexible when you don't resist the changes that God offers you. Instead, you see them as opportunities to obey Him, and you will grow closer to Him and discover that those weren't just changes—they were blessings.

Lord, help me be willing to follow you even if it involves making a life change.

- Tell about a time when God asked you to be flexible.
- Why did Abram choose to be flexible when God spoke to him?

Be Flexible

"For I know the plans I have for you," declares the LORD,
"plans to prosper you and not to harm you,
plans to give you hope and a future."

"I was studying engineering when I felt encouraged to explore beyond my plans," Carl explained to Pete.

"Why would God want you to leave college?" Pete had strong opinions about education.

"I knew I wasn't special in the classroom. I wasn't even that good. Then one day, at a car dealership, I recognized my gift for selling cars. God absolutely led me into that discovery."

"So you just switched career paths?"

Carl nodded. "Now I'm a manager of three dealerships, I have time to mentor high school kids, and I lead this Bible study."

Flexibility demonstrates the capacity to incorporate God's designs into our own lofty plans. Grace allows us to practice this skill, even when we don't get it right. When we adopt a rigid attitude about our hopes, we eschew the opportunity for God to bless us with a better plan.

If we can be flexible in all things, disappointment can be turned to victory. There is much in this world that we do not control, but a flexible person finds happiness and grace in change.

Lord, help me to be always open to your grace.

- Name one time when your rigid expectations caused you disappointment that could have been avoided.
- Why is God's agenda better than yours?

Annotations

Being flexible contributes to a joyful lifestyle and opens the way for God to bring great blessings in your life.

....
....
....
....
....
....
....
....
....
....
....
....
....
....
....
....
....
....
....
....
....
....
....
....
....
....
....

Reverence
and
Respect

Week
24

Something of Value

"Where your treasure is, there your heart will be also."
MATTHEW 6:21 NKJV

*V*alentine's Day had finally arrived! Suzanne's boyfriend made the day special for her. He'd arranged with her mom to bring heart-shaped biscuits for breakfast with Suzanne's family. After he left, she discovered a box of candy with her name on it.

An hour later, heart-shaped balloons arrived, and when Josh came to take her to dinner, he had a bouquet of lovely peach-colored roses—her favorite—and a beautifully wrapped box. When she opened it, the gift made her cry because it was a new Bible with a note written inside: *You're God's best gift to me. I prayed for someone special, and I'm so grateful for a girlfriend who will study God's Word with me.* It was obvious that he treasured her.

Suzanne's older sister, Kelly, also started the day with excitement, but disappointment soon followed. Her boyfriend sent no box of candy or flowers, and he didn't even call her. He had a habit of failing to show up for their dates, always with an excuse that made Kelly feel second-class.

Suzanne hugged Kelly. As Kelly cried, Suzanne silently wished her sister understood that she deserved someone who respected her.

Lord, help me to be an example of your love and to treat others with respect.

- How did Suzanne's boyfriend treat her with reverence and respect?
- Why is it important to have reverence and respect in our relationships?

Boomerang Love

This is My commandment,
that you love one another as I have loved you.

JOHN 15:12 NKJV

There are numerous varieties of love: the love of a mother for her child, the love between siblings (even though you sometimes hate to admit it), the love for a good friend, and the love God has for us, just to name a few.

Suzanne's boyfriend treated her with reverence and respect because he cared for her. In a sense, he couldn't help himself. Suzanne's happiness was that important to him, and he enjoyed finding ways to make her smile. When you revere someone, you value and cherish them, respecting them and placing their needs before your own.

There's a beautiful element to love: when we selflessly give it away, it often returns to us like a perfectly thrown boomerang. That's where we're wise to treat others as we want to be treated. Suzanne developed the habit of doing fun things to bring joy to her boyfriend too.

However, disrespecting others—as we learned from Kelly's experience—causes unnecessary pain. That's where today's verse comes into play. God loves us with a perfect love, and calls on us to love others in the same manner. To love, we must treat people with reverence and respect.

Father, help me to love like you do, and help me to bring joy into the lives of others.

- Why did Suzanne's boyfriend treat her with reverence and respect?
- Do you give love freely or are there strings attached?

When Love Began

Not looking to your own interests but each of you
to the interests of the others.

PHILIPPIANS 2:4

*R*uth was a young widow, but instead of staying with her people in Moab, she chose to accompany her despondent widowed mother-in-law, Naomi, back to Naomi's home country. In that town lived a wealthy man named Boaz.

Ruth and Naomi were poor, but Jewish law allowed those in want to glean the leftovers of the harvest from the fields—that which was not collected by the workers or was dropped by accident. Barley harvest had just begun, so Ruth went to Boaz's field of to gather what the reapers had neglected.

Boaz noticed Ruth in the field. His workers explained who she was and mentioned that she'd been out there working hard since morning. Boaz respected her work ethic and was touched by her loyalty and kindness to her widowed mother-in-law. He talked to her and shared his meal, then told Ruth to continue gleaning in his fields, where she would be safe, and to get water whenever she needed it.

He instructed his men to treat her well and to leave behind extra grain for her. A beautiful love story started that day, one that began with respect and reverence—a good starting point for any relationship.

Lord, help me to respect others and to treat my relationships with reverence.

- Why did Boaz respect Ruth?
- How did he treat her with reverence?

Thursday

A Love That Lasts

Beloved, let us love one another, for love is of God.

1 JOHN 4:7 NKJV

*J*osh enjoyed going all out when it came to his Valentine's Day acts of love because he respected Suzanne and wanted to make her feel special. Boaz made Ruth's life easier because he revered her. True love and respect ensues when we care more for others than we do for ourselves. Love is like a hungry bird. It must be fed often to keep it alive.

One reason Josh showed Suzanne such devotion was because of his great-grandparents. They'd been married for sixty-five years. Josh had grown up witnessing their care for each other. Gram would make dinner, and Gramps always complimented Gram on her cooking after the meal. Once he retired, Gramps insisted on doing the dishes each night to spare her bad back. They delighted in constantly caring for each other. Others found it remarkable when they witnessed their lasting love story and profound provision for each other after so many years of marriage. Josh understood it grew from a mutual, undying respect and reverence.

To build a love that lasts, start by looking at Jesus. Then look for friends who treat others with respect and kindness. Emulate their good traits. Become the person who will be that good example for others.

Father, thank you for your example of perfect love. Help me to extend that love to others.

- What can we learn from God's perfect love?
- What relationship have you observed that you want to emulate?

A Love to Give Away

Beloved, if God so loved us,
we also ought to love one another.

1 JOHN 4:11 NKJV

*R*omance need not be restricted to Valentine's Day. It's nice to make big gestures and give lovely gifts, but how we live in the everyday moments speaks to our character. We ought to treat each other with love and respect all the time. That should become ingrained in our character.

Look for little ways to show you care. Verbalize the words *I love you* rather than just expecting the other person to assume that you love them. There's a need in all of us to hear those words. Endeavor to be thoughtful without expecting anything in return. Offer encouragement with your words and actions.

The story of Ruth and Boaz provides some powerful guidelines. He may have noticed her looks, but he respected her character, her kindness, and her work ethic. Because he revered her, he made sure she would be safe and treated well, instructing his men to leave extra grain behind for her. Eventually, Boaz married Ruth.

Although Naomi had initially believed that God had forsaken her when her husband and sons were lost, in the end this beautiful love story proves God's provision and enduring devotion for her too.

Father, open my eyes to ways I can show reverence and respect to those I love.

- Why didn't Boaz just give the grain to Ruth?
- How can you invest in your relationships?

Annotations

Love is the engine that drives reverence and respect, and when we attempt to love like God does, we'll discover a new depth of reverence and respect for others.

Responsibility
and
Accountability

Freedom for All

"If the Son sets you free, you will be free indeed."

JOHN 8:36

In his "Summary View of the Rights of British America" in July 1774, Thomas Jefferson said, "The God who gave us life, gave us liberty at the same time." Jefferson recognized that being born into this life was a gift from God. He also acknowledged that this new country's government should primarily protect the freedom that comes from God.

God granted us "life, liberty, and the pursuit of happiness," as the United States Declaration of Independence says, through His Son, who came to bear witness to the Truth. There's also a responsibility that accompanies those blessings. We have an accountability to God and to our country.

Brandon learned that he could combine both of those responsibilities by volunteering after school for a political candidate who, if elected, would work hard to preserve the Judeo-Christian values this country was founded upon. Brandon stuffed envelopes, put out yard signs, and answered phones. He fulfilled his responsibility to be a good citizen *and* an involved Christian.

Lord, thank you for the freedom I have in you.

- Who is your favorite president of the United States and why?
- Celebrating President's Day gives us the opportunity to thank God for our heritage. Why is that important?

Do Your Part

For each one should carry their own load.

GALATIANS 6:5

When Sally, Jake, and Rich came home from school, they found a note from their mom. Please do your chores. Tonight will be family movie night if everyone does their jobs. Sally—clean bathrooms, Jake—sweep and mop floors, Rich—collect clothes and start the laundry.

The children busied themselves with chores. However, Jake got distracted, and when Mom got home, the floors weren't clean.

"But you said we could go to the movies," Jake whined when Mom's inspection found undone work.

"Yes, I did," she said, "but that was conditional. Look at the floors."

"But, Mom—"

"You didn't earn movie night, Jake. Now you have to stay home and sweep and mop the floors."

"I'm sorry, Mom," Jake said. "I'll do better next time."

Just as Mom trusted the kids with their responsibilities so she could treat them to a movie later, God trusts us to do things for Him. We are His hands and feet on this earth.

Sometimes we have to ask for God's forgiveness when we don't fulfill our responsibilities like loving others, sharing His story, showing kindness, and more. Make today a good day by finishing the tasks God gives you to do.

Lord, help me to honor you by fulfilling my responsibilities.

- Share about a time when you did not fulfill your responsibilities and it affected others.
- What is the best thing to do when your mom gives you a list?

Don't Pass the Buck

When Pilate saw that he was getting nowhere,
but that instead an uproar was starting, he took water
and washed his hands in front of the crowd. "I am innocent
of this man's blood," he said. "It is your responsibility!"

MATTHEW 27:24

"*P*assing the buck" is a phrase we often hear when someone intends to shift responsibility for something to someone else. Pilate passed the buck when he washed his hands of the blood of Jesus. He didn't want to be accountable for crucifying an innocent man.

Pilate offered to release one of the worst criminals of the land, Barrabas, in Jesus' place, obviously hoping the spectators would come to their senses and choose Jesus over Barrabas, but that didn't happen. Instead of endorsing the action of the crowd, and upon the pleading of his wife, Pilate attempted to remove himself from the situation, transferring responsibility onto the crowd. Of course, his very act of shifting blame acknowledged his power and accountability in this case. Think about that for a moment.

As believers, God has called us to a life of responsibility. We may not be workers in high government who make decisions that affect thousands of people, but every choice we make affects at least one person. Even if you are the only one involved, make good decisions to honor God and his gift of freedom.

Lord, help me to step up and meet the responsibility you give me.

- Are there times when it is okay to pass the responsibility to someone else? When?
- How do you feel when you are responsible for something really big?

Who Is Watching You?

In everything set them an example by doing what is good.
In your teaching show integrity, seriousness and soundness
of speech that cannot be condemned.

TITUS 2:7–8

M artin loved to shoot hoops in his neighbor's driveway. Often the younger boys joined him. One day, Martin took a moment away from his basketball game and shot the ball at the tender daffodil that had just pushed through the ground in Mrs. Dentuk's garden. Of course, it broke.

He resumed shooting hoops as Todd walked up. He threw the ball to him, and instead of shooting toward the hoop, Todd turned to the flower bed and threw the ball, crushing another of the flowers.

Martin felt bad. He'd led Todd astray. He called him over. "You know, Todd, those flowers are important to Mrs. Dentuk. I was wrong in shooting the ball at them, and I was a bad example to you. Please forgive me. I'm going to try really hard to set a good example and be accountable to you."

No matter your age, you are setting an example for someone. Someone in your class, on your team, or in your neighborhood is looking up to you. Whether you realize it or not, you are accountable to that person.

Lord, help me to be a good example to those watching me.

- How can you be a better example for others?
- Why is it important to be accountable to others?

Follow Jesus

"I have set you an example that you
should do as I have done for you."

JOHN 13:15

*A*s Christians, our goal should be to live more like Jesus every day. Studying His Word and learning from the way He loved and acted toward people, we should feel an increased yearning to act the same way.

Jesus always seemed to have time for those around him. He was never too busy to stop and heal someone, raise someone from the dead, or have a leisurely meal with friends. His mission focus was to help others.

On one occasion, someone touched the hem of Jesus' cloak. He felt the power go out of Him and stopped to inquire who might have touched Him. When the woman fell at His feet, Jesus granted her total healing.

People today are busy. Nobody likes to be interrupted when they're in the middle of something important, but Jesus never looked at these occurrences as interruptions. He saw them as opportunities to help someone or as chances to further the kingdom of God.

Jesus' example for us was a lifestyle of love, and He told us He was to be our example. It's our responsibility to keep following Him.

Lord, help me follow Jesus' example in every way. Help me to remember that I'm accountable for how I live each day.

- When was the last time you were interrupted to help someone? How did you respond?
- What other examples did Jesus establish for you to follow?

Annotations

The most important things are to be accountable to God and to be reliable in following the example of His Son, Jesus.

....
....
....
....
....
....
....
....
....
....
....
....
....
....
....
....
....
....
....
....
....
....
....
....
....
....
....

Dependability and and Reliability

Week 26

Not Again!

He who began a good work in you will bring it
to completion at the day of Jesus Christ.

PHILIPPIANS 1:6 ESV

*L*ucas sat with his head in his hands. "Why did I do that?"

He had trusted Tom with his family's secret, that his family was moving. Dad had asked that no one else know until his transfer was official, but Lucas told Tom. Tom told Lydia, Lydia told Frannie, and on and on. Obviously, Tom was not as dependable as Lucas thought, but Lucas had also betrayed his father's trust.

Dad sat on the step beside Lucas. "Son, I know you didn't mean to cause harm. You told Tom because you trusted him. But I depended on you to keep our secret."

"I just didn't understand why it was important to keep it a secret."

"Think about that for a minute, Lucas. Does it matter why I wanted it kept quiet?"

Lucas shrugged. "I guess not. You trusted me and I let you down."

"I hope you and Tom will learn from this. Dependability is a growth process, and this is a big lesson. Are you going to let this happen again?"

"No, sir. Thank you for the grace."

There's only one individual we can depend upon one hundred percent of the time. That's our heavenly Father. That's one reason we should always seek to emulate Him, and encourage others to do the same.

Lord, help me learn to be dependable.

- Why should we try to emulate God?
- Name three ways you can be a dependable friend.

Don't Lose Focus

I had planted you like a choice vine of sound
and reliable stock. How then did you turn
against me into a corrupt, wild vine?

JEREMIAH 2:21

*D*id you know that if left unpruned, many vines will become
unruly and wayward? The vine may appear strong and
sturdy and to follow a straight path, but if left unattended, it will
go its own way, usually an untidy, haphazard one.

The Israelites were kind of like that. God led them through
the wilderness, proffering miraculous provisions from heaven, but
despondency overwhelmed them. In the beginning, they relied
on God and His wisdom. They depended on Him for guidance.
Then their faith wavered and became inconsistent, then almost
nonexistent. They exchanged their loving God for idols. What a
terrible way to show their thanks!

This doesn't happen just in biblical times. Today people find
themselves close to God, walking with Him, and then they stray.
They may know in their hearts what the straight and right way
for dependence on God is, but they follow the way of the world.

Take a look at your relationship with God. Don't let it turn
into a wild vine.

Lord, help me to stand firm in the spot you have made for me.

- Is there some area of your life where you used to be
  strong and now you find yourself being inconsistent and
  wayward? How can you return to dependability?
- How do you feel when you know God cannot rely on
  you?

Reliable David

So Achish called David and said to him,
"As surely as the LORD lives, you have been reliable, and
I would be pleased to have you serve with me in the army.
From the day you came to me until today, I have found
no fault in you, but the rulers don't approve of you."

1 SAMUEL 29:6

*W*hen the Philistines gathered their forces at Aphek, David and his men marched at the end of the troops with Achish. The Philistine commanders became angry and were worried that David would turn against them, but David didn't want to leave. He questioned Achish and expressed his desire to help win the battle.

Achish answered with the words in today's verse, speaking to David's reliability. However, because the rulers didn't approve, Achish told David and his men to go home the next morning.

David was reliable and dependable. He did what was necessary to be a good warrior in this situation. God had other plans than for him to fight in this battle, so he had to return home.

David depended on God and trusted Him as he returned to the land of the Philistines. Sometimes we do the best we can in situations and feel like the outcome is not what we wanted, but our job is to be faithful and dependable in everything, even if our paths are redirected.

Lord, help me to be reliable and dependable.

- How would you feel in David's situation?
- Why should we act reliably in all situations?

God's Timing

For the word of the Lord holds true,
and we can trust everything he does.

PSALM 33:4 NLT

*F*rank looked at his grandfather's clock proudly displayed on the mantle. *I love this old clock.* He sighed as he ran his hand over the curved walnut, remembering his grandfather doing the same.

The clock was indeed beautiful. It had been well cared for and looked in perfect condition, at least on the outside. Despite its beauty, the clock really wasn't worth a whole lot. The timing mechanism was off, and even though Frank had taken the clock to several expert clock repairmen, it had never kept time well.

Even if the clock worked at the repair shop, by the time Frank brought it home, it was off by several minutes. Frank's family enjoyed the clock even though it chimed at odd intervals. The family often enjoyed a chuckle at the clock's expense. Someone would shout, "It must be seven and a half minutes after!" This old clock was dependably undependable.

We never have to question God's dependability or His timing. He will never be seven minutes past the correct time for anything. He will always be right on time. He is reliable in every situation, and you will never have cause to worry.

Lord, thank you for your dependability.

- Tell about a time when your dependability made a difference for someone.
- Name some people you know you can rely on, and note what other godly characteristics they exhibit.

Please Show Up

The works of his hands are faithful and just;
all his precepts are trustworthy.

PSALM 111:7 ESV

*H*annah and her Sunday school class planned to help an elderly church member dust and vacuum on Saturday morning. When Mrs. Hawkins asked for volunteers, over half of the girls raised their hands. "We'll have fun helping Mrs. Shaw get her home cleaned up!" Mrs. Hawkins said.

Saturday morning came, and Hannah and Mrs. Hawkins were the only ones who showed up. They worked hard and restored order and shine to much of the small house. However, they didn't get as much done as they had hoped, and it took longer than they had planned. If everyone who volunteered had come, they would have been finished quickly and completely, but the others were not dependable. Although Hannah and Mrs. Hawkins were disappointed, they did have a wonderful, blessed time together with Mrs. Shaw.

We often have the opportunity to show our dependability at home. What happens when you are asked to do the dishes, unload the dryer, clean the bathrooms, or do some other job? Do you busy yourself with other things, or do you realize that the request for your labor represents an opportunity to exhibit reliability, assist your family and please the heart of God?

Dependability is a trait that will serve you well for the rest of your life.

Lord, help me to always be dependable and to keep my word.

- Tell about a time when you weren't dependable, and let someone down.
- What are some of the ways you show you are dependable every day?

Annotations

No matter what work you hope to accomplish, being reliable and dependable will make you stand out in the crowd.

Contentment
and
Fulfillment

Week
27

Blessed

For I have learned in whatever state I am, to be content.

PHILIPPIANS 4:11 NKJV

*R*achel was on her first mission trip, and while Costa Rica was beautiful and the people were precious, she was stunned by the poverty she saw.

One day her group traveled to a village to work on a building project and conduct a service to share about God's love. Everyone on the bus was laughing until they got their first look at the village, and then silence reigned. The homes were odd-sized rickety shacks constructed of recycled, decrepit metal and wood. Hundreds of them were on the muddy hillside, mere feet from each other. There was no running water and no septic system. The families had minimal possessions, and most of what they had were things others had thrown away. Some didn't even have enough dishes for all the family members to eat at the same time.

What struck Rachel was that she didn't hear one bit of complaining or whining. The people were content with what they had. When the man who owned the shack they were in prayed over the sandwiches they'd brought with them, sincerely thanking God for how He'd blessed them, it moved Rachel to tears. She felt ashamed about all the times she'd complained about what she had or been envious of others.

Lord, teach me to be content.

- Why aren't we content with what we have?
- What did Rachel learn from the shack owner?

Tuesday

Abundance

A sound heart is life to the body,
But envy is rottenness to the bones.

PROVERBS 14:30 NKJV

That week, Rachel and the other members of the mission team learned several lessons that will stay with them for the rest of their lives. They realized that contentment comes from inside, and fulfillment comes in helping others, in serving God in ways that take us out of our comfort zones. For the first time, they truly recognized how much God had blessed them and how abundant their lifestyle was compared to many others in the world.

Rachel thought about that a lot on her flight home. She realized that she'd often been guilty of discontentment. She was ashamed as she thought about all the times she'd griped because her parents wouldn't buy her a designer handbag or when she'd complained that she didn't have the fashionable outfits she saw on others. She'd been guilty of coveting what other people had, and not appreciating the blessings she was already enjoying.

Until this trip, she'd never stopped to consider how fortunate she was to have a warm, leak-proof home, to have enough dishes and silverware at dinnertime, and to have a pantry and refrigerator overflowing with food.

Rachel had gone on this trip to bless others, but instead, *her* heart was the one that was touched the most.

Lord, remind me of my blessings.

○ Why do we often covet what others have?
○ What blessings do you need to thank God for today?

Whine, Whine, Whine

But if we have food and clothing,
we will be content with that.

1 TIMOTHY 6:8

*M*oses was over it. He'd listened to the children of Israel whine about their hardships until it was driving him crazy. Even God was so tired of listening to them that He sent fire from heaven to consume part of their camp.

Then they whined about the manna God sent them. "Why did we leave Egypt?" they murmured, dreaming about the days when they had meat, cucumbers, and melons, when they could flavor their food with leeks, garlic, and onions.

Moses listened to their grumbling until he'd had it. He told God, *What have I done to deserve this? Why have you burdened me with these whining people? If I have to put up with this rubbish from them much longer, just go ahead and kill me.*

No contentment was to be found in their camp. Yet, ironically, they were on their way to the Promised Land, where their dreams would be fulfilled. God had given them everything they'd need for the journey. He'd provided sustenance and someone to lead them, but they didn't recognize the blessings they had, so they whined.

I suspect many of us are probably shaking our heads in disbelief about how they acted, but how do *we* act when God doesn't give us exactly what we want?

Father, help me not to whine.

- Why did the children of Israel complain?
- Why was Moses tired of hearing it?

Like Milk and Cookies

I will be fully satisfied as with the richest of foods;
with singing lips my mouth will praise you.

PSALM 63:5

*A*lthough it's a wonderful thing to do, we don't have to go on a mission trip to another country to help others—or to learn valuable lessons about contentment.

Contentment and fulfillment go together like milk and cookies. When we're content with what we have, then we feel fulfilled—and when we take our eyes off ourselves and our petty wants, and gaze upon others who are in need, we'll find purpose and joy in a way we wouldn't have otherwise. We see our blessings with new eyes.

When our hearts are satisfied, then we'll praise Him, and when we're content with the blessings He's provided for us, we'll spare everyone else from having to put up with a whiny, grumpy, complaining person. Remember Paul and Silas, singing and praising God in chains, and how it affected those around them in the prison? Let's not forget that others are watching us each day, because when we respond to life with contentment and joy, we'll draw others to God.

Ask God to give you a deep compassion and a contentment with what you have, and to open your eyes to the ways that you can bless others. Practice being grateful.

Father, give me a content and joyful spirit that will draw others to you. Help me to see my blessings with new eyes.

- How can you determine to have a contented heart?
- How can your contentment and fulfillment affect others?

Contented

But godliness with contentment is great gain.

1 TIMOTHY 6:6

A contented spirit will bless you throughout your life. You'll be less likely to be in debt because you won't be constantly stretching your finances to procure a nicer car, bigger house, or finer jewelry.

Nobody likes to be around envious, whining, or ungrateful people. Contentment will take your eyes off yourself and put them on God and others. That's where true fulfillment is found.

There are many ways to accomplish that shift. Serve God by looking for opportunities to volunteer at your church or at a local ministry. Helping others will make you feel good, and you'll make new friends with similar values.

Ask God to give you a heart and spirit that is sensitive to the needs of others, and then when He spotlights those needs, spring into action. Maybe it's babysitting for a single mom so she can have a much-needed evening out or can go to buy groceries by herself. Consider washing the car or changing the oil for a senior citizen, or playing ball with the little boy down the street who doesn't have a dad to teach him how to play. Remember, being in service to others sometimes means setting aside your own ego. It's refreshing, and helps you tackle your own problems from a new perspective.

Ask God to generate a giving heart in you. When your focus is on doing for others, your own needs and wants take a back seat, and miraculously, you become more content!

Father, help me to focus on others.

- Why are godliness and contentment a great gain?
- How can serving others make us content?

Annotations

There's a deep joy that comes from being content—and when that contentment and joy overflows into the lives of others, *we* end up being the ones who are blessed.

Endurance and Fortitude

Week 28

Wasting Our Talents

"When someone has been given much, much will be
required in return; and when someone has been entrusted
with much, even more will be required."

LUKE 12:48 NLT

"I quit!" Maggie was so frustrated that she threw the paintbrush
into the trash can.

From the time she was a little girl working on her first paint-by-
number picture, she'd been fascinated by painting. Her teachers
had always commented about how talented she was. When her
mom bought two huge boxes of art supplies at a yard sale, Maggie
was excited. She knew immediately what she would paint. She
had an awesome photo of their church, and it would make a great
painting to give her pastor for Clergy Appreciation Sunday.

Maggie pulled out one of the canvas pieces and set it up on
an easel. She couldn't wait to get started, but an hour later, when
the painting didn't look like what she'd imagined, she threw the
paintbrush in the trash and quit. She had no endurance, and she
didn't have the fortitude to keep on at the task when it became
difficult.

Maggie wasted the money her mother had spent on her gift,
and even worse, she wasted the talent that God had given her—
because she wasn't willing to keep trying when the going got
tough.

Lord, help me to use all the talents you've given me.

- Why shouldn't Maggie have quit?
- What might she have done instead of throwing away
  the paintbrush?

Tuesday

Using Our Talents

And whatever you do, do it heartily,
as to the Lord and not to men.

COLOSSIANS 3:23 NKJV

Instead of having the endurance to see her painting through to the end, Maggie allowed frustration to discourage her.

A number of negative things happened because she quit. She disappointed herself because she'd desired to create a beautiful painting. She wasted the money her mother had spent on the art supplies—something her mom had done out of love for her daughter. Because Maggie gave up, her pastor wouldn't get a lovely painting of their church for Clergy Appreciation Sunday, and Maggie set a bad example for her younger siblings.

The saddest thing of all was that because Maggie didn't have the fortitude to finish the project, she wasted the talents that God gave her.

God gives unique gifts and talents to each of us, and He has plans for our lives that will use the talents that He's built into us—if we'll let Him. Some of us have talents for building things or conducting out-of-the-box science experiments. Other don't have those talents. Today would be a good time to reflect on the talents God has given you, to ask Him how you can use them for Him, and to dedicate yourself to fulfilling, with endurance, His expectations for you.

Lord, when challenges arrive, help me to respond with fortitude.

- What were the repercussions when Maggie quit?
- Why is it important for us to remain faithful even when the going gets tough?

God's Hall of Fame

Now faith is the substance of things hoped for,
the evidence of things not seen.

HEBREWS 11:1 NKJV

*E*ndurance and faith often go hand in hand. Sometimes we evaluate the tasks in front of us and fail to envision accomplishing them: that's relying on our own strengths. When we add faith and fortitude to the mix, we lean on God for His strength.

In Hebrews 11, sometimes called "God's Hall of Fame," it lists men and women who endured, who had the faith and fortitude to achieve what God asked them to do.

Here is what happened because of their endurance. Abel gained a testimony that he was righteous. Enoch gained a reputation that he pleased God. Noah is remembered as a man who feared God, building an ark for a circumstance he'd never seen—but saving his family as a result. When God told him to move, Abraham departed, not even knowing where he was going. It was enough that God had told him to do it. Sarah believed God—even when He gave her news that seemed impossible. The list in this chapter goes on and on, and all of these people obtained a good testimony because they endured.

Endurance is the ability to persevere, and fortitude is that tenacity strengthened by faith.

Father, give me a faith that will endure.

- What can we learn from the people in Hebrews 11?
- Why do you think they were so faithful?

The Endurance Award

For you have need of endurance, so that after you have
done the will of God, you may receive the promise.

HEBREWS 10:36 NKJV

Sometimes we can't envision the end result of what we do
for God. The men and women in Hebrews 11 received the
promise from God of what He was going to do, but some didn't
live long enough to see the outcome. Their faith taught them
that if God makes a promise, He will fulfill it.

When we're young children and we sell candy bars or calen-
dars as a fund-raiser, we work hard because we've seen the list of
possible rewards and we want that bicycle or that three-foot-tall
candy bar. Sometimes doing things for God doesn't work that
way, however. Instead, doing His will is its own reward. Our
endurance and fortitude to complete His plans then lead to mer-
iting His promises, some of which we've already received.

Has God placed something on your heart that He wants you to
do, but it seems impossible? That's not a problem, because nothing is impossible for Him. He will equip you with the skills, the
knowledge, the tools you need, and others who can help you. All
He needs from you is a willing heart that will endure to the end.

**Lord, help me to stop looking at my lack of abilities and to
envision what you can do.**

- Why can we count on God when He makes us a
  promise?
- What does He want/need from us?

Don't Miss the Moments

Be steadfast, immovable, always abounding
in the work of the Lord, knowing that your
labor is not in vain in the Lord.

1 Corinthians 15:58 NKJV

When it comes to serving God, one of the biggest hurdles can be taking that first step of faith. Fear can hold us back from accomplishing God's plans, so we need to conquer it, then work with endurance until the task is completed.

For the men and women who are listed in Hebrews 11, it was enough that God told them to do something. Even though other people didn't understand what they were doing—and sometimes *they* didn't even understand why God had asked them to do it—they worked with faithful fortitude to complete the tasks God had assigned to them.

As Clergy Appreciation Sunday approached, Maggie started feeling bad about not finishing her painting. She put the canvas back on the easel and started painting again—but this time she prayed first and said, "God, give me the fortitude to finish this. Help it to be an encouragement for my pastor."

On the day she presented the painting to him, her pastor was so touched that he teared up. Wouldn't it have been a shame for her to have missed that moment? What moments like that are *you* missing out on, because you gave up too soon?

Father, give me a heart of endurance.

- How does fear hold us back from serving God?
- How can our visible endurance affect others?

Annotations

Endurance paired with faith makes an unbeatable combination. When we have the fortitude to complete the tasks God gives us to do, we please His heart.

Sensitivity and Sympathy

Week
29

A Sensitive Heart

As each one has received a gift,
minister it to one another.

1 PETER 4:10 NKJV

*J*ustin's mom, Donna, had became a single parent four years earlier when his dad died. She worked long hours, but finances were still tight. She was a great mom, and it made him sad the day he realized that she never spent any money on herself. Her clothes came from consignment shops, and she never had matching accessories like many of the other moms at church, so Justin hatched a plan.

He saved the money he got from his grandparents for Christmas, he did chores for his neighbors to earn some extra money, and he saved the cash from his birthday gifts. Finally, he reached the goal he'd set.

Justin's aunt went to the mall with him and helped him find a beautiful dress for his mom in her favorite color. They picked out jewelry, stylish shoes, and a matching handbag—one he'd seen his mom glance at wistfully the last time they were at the department store.

The week before Easter, he handed his mom four beautifully wrapped packages. She cried as she opened them. She loved the gifts, but what touched her most was Justin's sensitive heart, that he'd loved her enough to do without things himself so she could have something special.

Father, give me a caring heart.

- Why did Justin do this for his mom?
- How does having a sympathetic heart make a difference?

Tuesday

Blessing Others

But do not forget to do good and to share,
for with such sacrifices God is well pleased.

HEBREWS 13:16 NKJV

*W*hen Justin crafted the plan to give his mom a beautiful
new outfit and accessories for Easter, he asked his sister,
Courtney, if she wanted to join in with him for the gift. She just
laughed at him and said, "Are you serious? I'm saving my money
to buy something nice for myself. Mom has never complained to
me about her clothes or her jewelry."

Courtney was often callous to the needs of others and exhibited an all-about-me mentality that was the opposite of Justin's
sensitivity. He had sympathy—a feeling of compassion and care
for his mom—but he also had empathy for her because he put
himself in her place and realized that she must want to look nice
and have something stylish to wear.

He did it for his mom, but the interesting thing was that his
project brought joy to several people. Donna was moved to happy
tears by his gesture, his aunt was touched by what Justin did and
thrilled to be called on to help out, and even Justin got a little
emotional as he saw his mom's reaction to her gift. Best of all, Justin's love and compassion for his mom pleased the heart of God.

God, as you bless me, help me to bless others.

- What did Justin's sister miss by not taking part in his gift?
- Why did Justin know what his mom wanted when his
  sister couldn't tell?

Wednesday

Because of Love

The king asked, "Is there no one still alive from the
house of Saul to whom I can show God's kindness?"

2 SAMUEL 9:3

*I*magine learning the news that your father and grandfather had
died, and then becoming lame in both feet all on the same day.
That would be rough at any age, but can you imagine how hard
that was for five-year-old Mephibosheth?

From then on, life was difficult for him in many ways—as a
child and also as an adult. He had no clue that his life would
change one day due to the sensitivity of a man who had loved his
father, but that's what happened.

David had been friends with Mephibosheth's father, Jonathan—close friends. Often, when a new king was crowned, he
removed everyone from the previous administration, but when
David was made king, he asked his servant if there was anyone
left of the household of Jonathan so he could show kindness to
them.

One of King Saul's servants told David about Jonathan's son,
Mephibosheth, who was lame in both feet. David summoned
him, and then, out of sympathy and because he'd loved Mephibosheth's father, David promised his old friend's son kindness and
hospitality. He restored the young man's land, and from then on,
Mephibosheth always ate at the king's table.

Lord, teach me to be sensitive to the needs of others.

- Why was David kind to Mephibosheth?
- How did that change Mephibosheth's life?

Gifts of Love

The generous soul will be made rich.

PROVERBS 11:25 NKJV

*J*ustin and King David were both sensitive to the needs of others, but what sets them apart as role models is that they each did something about it.

In Justin's case, it required sacrificing his own desires so he could bless his mother instead. He had a purpose and a plan.

David also *looked* for ways he could bless others. His friend Jonathan had been loyal to him—and David remembered that and wanted to pay it forward. He had the power and means to make Mephibosheth's life better, and he took pleasure doing it.

When Donna wore the lovely outfit from her son, she felt wrapped in her son's love. She felt special each time she wore it, knowing it was given sacrificially from his heart. That moment happened many years ago. Justin's mom had recently died, and when he went through a trunk in the attic, he found the outfit carefully packed in a box. However, it was the note inside in his mom's handwriting that made tears well up in his eyes, because it said, *A gift of love from my son.*

You'll never regret being kind and compassionate to others.

Lord, help me to be sensitive to the needs of others, and dispense kindness every day.

- How does being sympathetic affect us and others around us?
- How can we look for ways to bless others?

Make Me a Blessing

Pleasant words are like a honeycomb,
Sweetness to the soul and health to the bones.

PROVERBS 16:24 NKJV

This week, Justin and David have provided great examples of how to seek a way to bless others sympathetically. Let's ask God to give *us* hearts that are sensitive to the needs of others. Start today with your teachers or your family. Maybe you could help clean up after class for your teacher, or volunteer to tutor someone who is struggling with their studies. Stepping up to do extra chores would give someone else the opportunity to sit down and rest for a few minutes.

We need to do what David did—to look for someone we can bless. People who need someone to love them or provide a helping hand are all around us. Maybe it's bringing a hot meal to your elderly neighbor. Perhaps it's calling your pastor and asking, "What can I do to help you today?"

We need to be willing to sacrifice. That can include our time, activities we want to do, or finances. We must also say the words that need to be said. Look for someone you can encourage. Comfort a hurting heart. Take time to tell someone about Jesus. Invite a friend to join you at church or youth group.

Make sympathy a part of every day.

Lord, help my actions and my words touch the lives of others.

- How can you look for ways to help others?
- How can you use words to bless someone?

Annotations

Sensitivity and sympathy are just words until we put them into action—but when we notice the needs of others and do something about them, we emulate God.

....
....
....
....
....
....
....
....
....
....
....
....
....
....
....
....
....
....
....
....
....
....
....
....
....
....

Forgiveness
and
Mercy

Week
30

Damaged

Get rid of all bitterness, rage and anger.

EPHESIANS 4:31

From the time he was a little boy, Mason had loved vehicles. On his tenth birthday, he told his dad, "I'm going to save my money so I can buy a truck when I turn sixteen." That's what he did, squirreling away the cash from his birthday and Christmas gifts, and money he made doing frequent yardwork for his neighbors.

He gained great satisfaction from watching the amount grow in his savings account. On the day he got his driver's license, he went with his dad to a car dealership and was able to pay for a newer-model used truck.

He *loved* that truck. It was black and sporty, and he kept it so polished you could see your reflection in it. Well, that's how it looked until the night Mason's older brother didn't see the truck in the driveway and backed into it, crumpling the side of it.

It was an accident, but Mason was so mad that he socked his brother in the nose. He'd worked hard to get that truck! For weeks, he didn't speak to his brother. He didn't even want to be in the same room with him.

His brother apologized repeatedly, and Mason's refusal to forgive his brother affected the whole family—but the person it hurt the most was Mason, as bitterness consumed him.

Lord, give me a forgiving heart.

- How did Mason's unforgiving heart affect his family?
- How did it affect him?

Sweet Forgiveness

The Lord our God is merciful and forgiving.

Daniel 9:9

*M*ason had worked hard to pay for his truck, and one can understand why he was upset when it was damaged. However, what he failed to see was that his unforgiving heart was even more damaged than his truck. Insurance would fix the truck, but he had caused damage to his relationship with his brother, leaving scars that would always be there for both of them.

Even after Mason's truck was repaired, home from the body shop, and looking brand-new, there were residual hidden damages that remained and festered. Mason had hurt his brother over a frivolous accident. His rejection and refusal to show mercy lodged a wedge in their relationship. He'd disappointed his parents, but most importantly, he'd grieved the heart of God.

The truck that had once given him so much joy when he looked at it now just brought heartache. Mason couldn't even sleep, because whenever he closed his eyes, it was as if he could hear God whisper, "I forgave *you*."

Finally, Mason did what he should have done at the beginning. He prayed, "God, help me to show mercy like you do." The next morning, he told his brother, "I'm sorry. I forgive you." The peace that flooded his soul was worth more than any truck that would ever sit in his driveway.

Father, thank you for your mercy.

- Why do our actions sometimes leave scars?
- How can we forgive like Jesus?

Undeserved

"But while he was still a long way off, his father saw him
and was filled with compassion for him."

LUKE 15:20

*J*esus shares a compelling story in Luke 15. A father had two sons, and when one of them asked for his share of his father's estate, the father gave portions to both sons.

The obedient son was wise with what he'd been given, but the other son took his new windfall, packed his belongings, and left home. He went wild, foolishly squandering his money. Right after he depleted his funds, a famine hit the land, and he was in such dire need that he took a job feeding the pigs.

The Prodigal Son was so hungry that he wanted to eat the pig's food. That was quite a change from his former lavish lifestyle. One day, when he scrutinized his unfortunate circumstances, he realized that even the servants at his father's house had food to eat.

He decided to go home, beg his father to forgive him, and ask for a job as one of his father's servants. Imagine how his stomach flip-flopped with nervousness as he neared home. He couldn't be certain what he would encounter when he got there, but certainly he imagined his own shame and humiliation and that his father be furious and disappointed. He envisioned his father just sending him away.

When he arrived, however, what he discovered was his father crying out with joy, offering forgiveness and mercy. Unexpected, undeserved, but graciously given.

Father, thank you for undeserved mercy.

- How did the Prodigal Son's choices affect him?
- Why did the father respond with mercy?

Mercy Is Waiting

"If you forgive other people when they sin against you,
your heavenly Father will also forgive you."

MATTHEW 6:14

We celebrate Easter around this time of year, and there's no better example of forgiveness and mercy than Jesus. Despite our flaws and failures, He looked at us through eyes of grace and loved us anyway. In fact, He loves us so much that He gave His life for us, taking the punishment in our place.

Mercy is not getting what you deserve. It forgives, pardons, and wipes away the indiscretions as if they'd never happened. Unlike Mason, who initially refused to forgive his brother, we can come to God and know that mercy is always awaiting our contrite hearts.

The father of the Prodigal didn't greet his younger son with anger and bitterness over how he had acted. Instead, likely reading the sorrow on his son's face, he met him with immediate mercy, wrapped his arms around him, and ordered the servants to prepare a fine meal. He mercifully accepted him back into the family.

Just as God forgives us, we also have a responsibility to forgive others—even when they don't deserve it.

Jesus painted a beautiful picture of that as He hung on the cross. Some people might think that the nails were what kept Him there, but it was really love and mercy.

Father, thank you for sweet forgiveness and for loving me no matter what.

- Why is it important for us to forgive?
- How do you think it made the Prodigal Son feel to be greeted with mercy?

Forgive Yourself

Therefore, having been justified by faith, we have peace
with God through our Lord Jesus Christ.

ROMANS 5:1 NKJV

The father of the Prodigal Son and Mason both granted forgiveness. That was a wonderful and loving thing for them to do, but there's another element of forgiveness that we haven't talked about yet—and that's forgiving ourselves.

We are sometimes our own worst enemies, beating up on ourselves, especially when we've done something that has hurt someone we love. The guilt of that can take root in our hearts and cause great anguish.

There are a couple of things that we can do that will help in this regard. We can turn the burden over to Jesus, telling Him how sorry we are and asking for His guidance to keep us from making that mistake again. We can also look for ways that we can make restitution to the person we've wronged. It won't wipe away the moment for which forgiveness was needed, but that gesture will demonstrate your repentant heart and your desire to make amends. The words *I'm sorry* go a long way when expressed sincerely and accompanied by an acknowledgment of the wrong we've done.

Grant yourself the same mercy you would give to someone else, and know that because of God's precious gift on Calvary, forgiveness and peace await you.

Father, thank you for the gift of Jesus, and for mercy and forgiveness.

- Why do we have trouble forgiving ourselves?
- Why do we have trouble asking for forgiveness from others, and from God?

Annotations

When we withhold forgiveness and mercy, it can lead to bitterness for us and scars for others. Forgiveness and mercy are often undeserved; they're manifestations of grace.

Gentleness and Tenderness

Week
31

Gentle or Tender

Let your gentleness be evident to all. The Lord is near.

PHILIPPIANS 4:5

*G*entleness and tenderness seem to be closely related words, even to the point of sometimes being interchangeable, but there is a difference. Gentleness is the physical manner in which something is approached. Tenderness is a matter of the heart.

Jesus was a master of gentleness, tenderness, and compassion. The shortest verse in the Bible, "Jesus wept" (John 11:35), shows us His tender heart upon the death of his good friend Lazarus and the tremulous disbelief of the mourners.

When Jesus arrived in Bethany after hearing of Lazarus' death, he was berated by both Mary and Martha because Lazarus had already been in the tomb for four days. Jesus' friends mourned and wept. Jesus was deeply moved, and He wept with them.

A tender heart is kind and considerate. A compassionate person displays empathy, sharing the pain or heartache of others as if it were one's own. When you feel yourself tearing up at a sweet song, a ball game victory, or the success of a friend, it is because your heart is tender and you care.

Jesus showed us that sad occasions often bring on emotions that spring from tender feelings. When you feel emotion inside, don't hide those feelings. Be like Jesus, and let the world see your tenderness.

Lord, keep my heart tender and my touch gentle.

- Why might you embarrassed if anyone saw you weeping?
- Why might it be hard to show compassion for some people?

An Unkind Outburst

The words of the reckless pierce like swords,
but the tongue of the wise brings healing.

PROVERBS 12:18

"Autumn, you're dumb. You're never going to pass this class."

"It was just one test, Grant. And I study, probably harder than—"

"Well, it doesn't look like you study very much," Grant interrupted. "You're a loser."

Autumn turned toward her locker. She knew she was a good student. A big tear trickled down her cheek, and then she felt a hand on her shoulder.

"I heard what Grant said. Don't believe him. You are a beautiful person, inside and out. And you're smart too." Heather gave Autumn a hug.

"Thanks. I know how Grant is, but it still hurts when he comes after me. I see him talk to others that way too."

"Well, don't listen to him. He's just jealous and insecure." Heather smiled. "Let's go to lunch and show Grant his words can't hurt you."

When Grant spoke unkind and harsh words to Autumn, he was saying more about himself than about her. Although his words hurt her feelings, Grant displayed his own shortcoming: his insensitive, cruel heart. Even worse, he grieved the heart of God.

Lord, keep me from hurtful outbursts at my family and friends.

- Have you ever had been unkind to someone, like Grant was? What was it about? What should you have done?
- What can you do when you feel yourself about to explode with unkind words?

The Fruit of Gentleness

But the fruit of the Spirit is love, joy, peace,
forbearance, kindness, goodness, faithfulness, gentleness and
self-control. Against such things there is no law.
Those who belong to Christ Jesus have crucified
the flesh with its passions and desires.

GALATIANS 5:22–24

*G*alatians lists the fruits of the Spirit. They are the evidence the Holy Spirit is living in you. Because of His presence in your life, you will develop character traits that will please Him.

The Gospel of Luke tells the story of a paralyzed man. His friends loved him and were concerned about his plight, and they heard Jesus was healing sick people.

One said, "We're going to take you to Jesus. He can heal you."

"Take me?"

"Yes, we will carry you."

His friends picked him up on his blanket and took him to where Jesus was speaking. The crowd was so large they could not get their friend to the door of the house, so they gently lowered him through the roof right to the feet of Jesus. Jesus told him his friends' faith had healed him. The result of their compassionate actions was that the man was able to walk again.

God gave this man friends who had tender hearts and compassion for him. When we show the gentleness of Jesus to our friends and others, it's as though we are extensions of God's hands.

Lord, develop strong character in me.

- How can the Holy Spirit produce fruit in your life?
- Name a time when you shared the spirit of gentleness.

Little Children, Come!

Therefore if you have any encouragement from being united
with Christ, if any comfort from his love, if any common
sharing in the Spirit, if any tenderness and compassion, then
make my joy complete by being like-minded, having the
same love, being one in spirit and of one mind.

PHILIPPIANS 2:1–2

*E*verywhere Jesus went, he had throngs of people around him. One time he was ministering in the marketplace and people brought their children to Jesus. The disciples, however, discouraged that. They might have said something like, "Can't you see Jesus is busy? Don't bother him with children."

Even so, Jesus quickly refuted them. In His tenderness and compassion, He gathered the little children to Him. He probably pulled some on His lap and reached out His arms to others. He began to love on them and said, "Let the children come." Close your eyes and picture lots of excited children jumping up and down, reaching out their arms to Jesus. Can't you just imagine them yelling, "Pick me, pick me, pick me!"

Jesus didn't see the children as an interruption. He saw them as an important part of the people who God sent Him to serve and love. He came to love us all—regardless of age, nationality, or gender.

Lord, help me to welcome all people.

- How do you suppose those children's parents felt about their children sitting with Jesus?
- How can you be more open to helping others around you? Could you volunteer to help people regularly?

Gentle Words

Always be prepared to give an answer to everyone
who asks you to give the reason for the hope that you have.
But do this with gentleness and respect.

1 PETER 3:15

In the Great Commission (Matthew 28:16–20), Jesus tells us to go to the world and share the gospel and that He will be with us. The *what*, *who*, and *where* are clear, but the *how* is found elsewhere in the Bible.

Peter tells us to always be prepared to share the hope of Jesus with gentleness and respect. That can apply to our interactions with our parents.

What if your mom comes into your room, finger pointing, and says with a raised voice, "You're so messy. Clean your room now. Do you hear me?" Do you feel like responding to that? Now what if she comes in with a smile and says, "Honey, there's a lot of stuff on the floor. Do you think maybe you could straighten up a bit? Let me know if I can help." Which method do you respond to best?

An old cliché says, "You can catch more flies with honey than with vinegar." When applied to our lives, that means, "You get better results speaking kindly to others."

Gentleness is like honey. When you tell someone about Jesus, speak in kind, gentle tones so it will be amiably received in a life-changing way.

Lord, help us to speak with gentleness.

- How might you improve the way you share your faith?
- How can speaking gently change family dynamics?

Annotations

Reaching the hearts of others is easier done with gentleness and tenderness. Gentle touches and words of kindness are always better received than a curt attitude.

....
....
....
....
....
....
....
....
....
....
....
....
....
....
....
....
....
....
....
....
....
....
....
....

Creativity
and
Vision

Week
32

Wasted Talents

Do not neglect the gift that is in you.

1 TIMOTHY 4:14 NKJV

*V*ince and Michael had been captivated by science from the time they were little guys and they saw the fizzy reaction between vinegar and baking soda. Through the years, they'd crafted bottle rockets, performed egg-drop contests, and created gooey slime. Their appreciation for science carried over into their teen years, and they enjoyed making up their own experiments.

They even built their own science lab in the detached garage, and spent hours out there pretending they were Einstein. Their mom purchased whatever they needed for their projects, recognizing that their delight in experimenting and researching was a gift from God.

Fast-forward twenty years. Vince had worked hard during that time, achieving top academic honors all the way through college. He had a solid plan, a strong vision of his future, and he worked diligently to make that happen. His degree led to a career in the research lab for a major pharmaceutical company.

Michael had goofed around and partied his way through high school. He didn't have the vision and foresight his brother had, and he wasted the creativity God had given him.

Let's determine today that we'll carefully plan, diligently execute, and faithfully employ all the gifts and talents God has provided for us.

Lord, let me make the most of the creative talents you've given me.

- What gifts and talents has God given you?
- Why should you aspire to use your creativity to the fullest?

God's Plan

All things were created through Him and for Him.

COLOSSIANS 1:16 NKJV

Have you ever watched thousands of snowflakes drifting down? Each of them is a one-of-a-kind creation—and we are as well. While we might resemble family members, none of us are exactly the same.

We have different life experiences and spiritual journeys, and because of that, God has designed us to accomplish tasks for Him that nobody else can fulfill. Sure, other people can come in and pick up the pieces if we fail to achieve to our potential, but we will have thwarted God's perfect vision for us.

Vince recognized that God had given him a talent for research and science, and he worked diligently to fill the role God had for him. Because of that, he completed research projects that would bring great relief to people suffering from a serious medical condition.

We can't talk about what Michael accomplished for the vision God had for his life because he didn't fulfill it. He might have discovered the cure for diabetes or glaucoma, but he didn't.

What are you doing with the creative gifts and talents God has given to you? Ask Him to show you what He wants you to do—because it would be a shame to stand before Him someday and say, "I wasted all of it."

Father, help me to fulfill your plan.

- What individual talents has God given you?
- What makes you a one-of-a-kind design?

A Creative God

*"Let Your servant prosper this day, I pray,
and grant him mercy in the sight of this man."*

NEHEMIAH 1:11 NKJV

*N*ehemiah was a cupbearer in the king's palace. When some men arrived from Judah, he asked how things were in Jerusalem. He was heartbroken to hear that the wall around the city had been torn down and the gates had been destroyed by fire.

A dream grew in his heart to restore the city. He prayed, asking for favor from the king as he presented his request to send him to Judah. Nehemiah asked for letters to the governors of other territories so he could travel safely, and he asked for supplies. In answer to Nehemiah's prayers, the king gave him more than he'd asked for, and Nehemiah left on his journey for God.

People laughed at him and tried to thwart his efforts, but his enthusiasm led to a multitude of the Jewish people springing into action to help rebuild Jerusalem. Because he'd inspired so many people, the wall was completed in only fifty-two days.

By one man's vision and his creativity in bringing that visualization to life, a city was restored—one that had been in complete ruin. One man's vision led to action from many others.

We've seen what Nehemiah did. Ask God to give you vision for what *you* can do for Him.

Lord, give me the vision to dream impossible dreams for you.

- What was impressive about Nehemiah's vision?
- How can our vision inspire others?

Thursday

By Design

When I consider Your heavens, the work of Your fingers,
The moon and the stars, which You have ordained,
What is man that You are mindful of him,
And the son of man that You visit him?

<small>PSALM 8:3–4 NKJV</small>

If you've ever been to Disney World, you were probably fascinated by the creativity of the people behind the rides and attractions. They had a crew of Disney Imagineers who designed what you see there, and thousands of people were involved in making their vision happen.

God is a one-man design team. He has a vision for His creation, and He takes satisfaction and pride in all that He makes—including you.

Sometimes as we seek to use our creativity and talent, we allow fear and insecurity to defeat us. We worry about our lack of skills instead of focusing on His abundance of abilities. If He calls us to a task, He will not leave us floundering. He will equip us with what we need, and will walk beside us every step of the way.

Don't get the mistaken idea that it will always be easy. There will be times of discouragement, moments when it seems like it's taking forever for things to happen, and there may even be times when you'll want to quit. However, the completion of your very own creative vision is an incredibly enticing incentive, and of course the reward of pleasing Him is always worth the effort.

Lord, help me to use my creativity for you.

- How does fear affect you?
- How do creativity and pleasing God fit together?

Well Done!

Give instruction to a wise man, and he will be still wiser;
Teach a just man, and he will increase in learning.

PROVERBS 9:9 NKJV

*G*od has wired us a certain way, and as you settle into the vision of life that He has for you, you'll discover He has already equipped you with the skills and talents you'll need to accomplish those tasks. All that creativity is there for a reason, so how can you discover His calling for you?

Invite your parents, teachers, pastor, and other people who know you well to tell you what gifts and talents they see in you. Often, people reflect to us a vision of ourselves we could never appreciate, alone. Try to see your talents through their eyes. Investigate which future career choices might benefit from your specific talents. Consider classes or courses you could take in those fields to help you prepare for what lies ahead. Develop a vision and a plan, but be prepared for God to send unexpected opportunities into your life.

Ask loved ones and your pastor to help you pray for guidance. Pray daily yourself and ask God to show you His vision for your future. Most of all, be sensitive to His leading.

Fulfill the plan that He has for you, because it would be so special to stand before Him someday and hear Him say, "Well done, good and faithful servant."

Lord, show me the plan you have for me, and teach me to be wise.

- Why is understanding your talents important?
- How can that knowledge affect your plans and your future?

Annotations

When we seek God's plan for using our creativity and talents, we can rest assured that He will provide all we need.

....
....
....
....
....
....
....
....
....
....
....
....
....
....
....
....
....
....
....
....
....
....
....
....
....

Meekness and Modesty

Week
33

Are You Meek?

"Blessed are the meek, for they will inherit the earth."

MATTHEW 5:5

One day, Geoff came outside to play catch with his brother on the cul-de-sac. Alex, the new neighbor, stood on his porch with his arms crossed, staring darkly.

"Want to catch the ball with us?" Geoff asked affably.

"Baseball is stupid," Alex scoffed. "I don't see why you even try. You're not very good."

"Well, luckily, we don't have to be pros to just have fun with it. You should try it sometime. It's fun!" Geoff added, laughing as he threw the ball.

"Throwing a dumb ball back and forth? I mean, what's the point?"

"It's good exercise too," added Donny, Geoff's younger brother.

"Shut up, Stupid! Nobody asked you," Alex taunted angrily.

Just then, Geoff caught the ball from Donny. "Hey! You don't speak to my brother like that, understood?" Geoff stood his ground with his hands on his hips. "You should apologize for that, Alex," he said softly.

It was a standoff, until Alex turned on his heel and went back inside.

Meek is not a common word, but it's in the Old and New Testament. The appropriate definition here is "power under control." Jesus chose His replies carefully. He quietly used His power to change lives. Follow Jesus' example of knowing His power and using it in an unassuming and quiet way. If we show others how to be meek—how to be strong instead of weak—our world will be better.

Lord, we need meekness in our world. Let it start with me.

- Why did Geoff respond with meekness?
- Tell about a time you acted meekly.

Tuesday

Modesty Wins

Who is wise and understanding among you?
Let him show by good conduct that his works
are done in the meekness of wisdom.

"Mom, why did you let Seth unload the dishwasher? I can't find anything. He doesn't know how to do it right. I know where everything goes. Nobody would have to look for anything."

"Yes, Trevor, you know where everything goes, and you do a great job. But Seth needs to learn how to do these things. And it doesn't help for you to badger him and act like a know-it-all."

"But, Mom—"

"You go clean the bathrooms. I'll finish the laundry, and then we can get outside and enjoy a walk."

Trevor's mom knew her oldest son was seldom pleased with his younger brother's work. Trevor was a perfectionist who struggled with restraint and assertiveness. She knew Seth needed to be encouraged in learning how to do his chores. As well, Trevor needed to learn how to be gentle with his words and advice.

Many people struggle with how to offer knowledge and opinions. Jesus gave a perfect example. He knew everything yet didn't push His knowledge on others at the wrong time. He used restraint, was meek, and treated others with kindness.

Lord, help me to realize I don't know everything. Help me to rely on you for my wisdom.

- What's one way you can you be more like Jesus?
- How could Trevor have helped Seth by employing meekness?

Meekness Honors God

Now the man Moses was very humble,
more than all men who were on the face of the earth.

NUMBERS 12:3 NKJV

*M*oses was meek above all men, yet God spoke to him face-to-face, entrusting him with the Ten Commandments. God relied on Moses because He knew his heart. He depended on him to be His messenger.

Riley was a messenger too. Even though her personality seemed reserved and she rarely instigated conversations, her life was a message. She had many opportunities to share her message with her friends, like the other day.

"Hey, Riley," Clint said. "Wanna come over tonight? We're going to party at my house. My parents will be out for the evening at a late event!"

"Do your folks know?"

"Not exactly, but they let me do what I want, anyway."

"Thanks for inviting me, but I don't think I should."

"Really? Don't you like fun?"

"Of course. But it sounds like you are dishonoring your folks. I'm a Christian, and I want to honor God with everything I do."

Riley had her priorities in order. She wanted to keep her testimony above reproach, and she knew how to share her reply meekly. When her opportunity came to speak, she did.

Moses showed power in his meekness. Riley did as well. Both honored God.

Lord, help me to honor you in everything I do.

- How would you react if your friends invited you to join in something questionable?
- Why was it important for Riley to explain her reasoning?

Meekness Is Powerful

"Take my yoke upon you, and learn from me, for I am gentle
and lowly in heart, and you will find rest for your souls."

MATTHEW 11:29 ESV

*J*esus entered the temple, He saw people buying and selling there, and his mood darkened. He told the people, "Is it not written: 'My house will be called a house of prayer ...'? But you have made it 'a den of robbers'" (Mark 11:17). His displeasure was obvious, and He took control of what was going on by overturning the tables. What an act of strength!

Jesus showed His power against the enemy. He demonstrated meekness as He entered the temple, pointed out the wrong that was going on, and did what was necessary to demonstrate for everyone God's displeasure at the sinful practice inside the temple. He left no doubt as to where he stood, and he showed power, under control.

Meekness should not be confused with shyness or aloofness. Meekness is a positive part of your personality that shows strength and humility. If you practice meekness, it will give way to a type of power that you probably weren't aware you possessed.

There are many ways to expose all the wrongs in the world today. If you act meekly yet boldly, you are acting as Jesus did.

Lord, use my meekness as a tool to bring others to you, and keep me from being boastful.

- In what ways do you show Jesus to your friends?
- How do you feel when you're around someone who's boastful?

Meek, Not Weak

But the meek will inherit the land
and enjoy peace and prosperity.

PSALM 37:11

*D*onny stood on the cul-de-sac in front of his house, tossing a baseball into his mitt and waiting for his brother Geoff to get off the phone. Alex sauntered out his front door, hands behind his back, glowering, as if he hadn't appreciated the confrontation with Geoff the day before. Donny watched him, cringing and feeling intimidated. He wished Geoff would get outside, *now*.

Alex said in a loud voice, "Not so tough now that big brother isn't around, are you?"

Donny had learned a bit from Geoff, though. He stood his ground, looked Alex in the eye, and shrugged his shoulders, all the while still tossing the ball into his glove. Just then, Geoff launched out the front door. He stopped short and surveyed the scene, then turned to Alex, waiting, and smiling in a friendly way.

Alex paused for a moment. "All right. I'm sorry for calling you stupid, Donny. I was in a bad mood. My mom says that moving is stressful."

Geoff and Donny both grinned. "Wanna play catch, then?" Donny asked. "You got a glove?" Alex pulled a glove out from behind his back, and Donny tossed him the ball. "Think fast!"

Geoff's calm and gentle spirit diffused the situation and turned it into a positive for everyone. Because Geoff showed the love of Jesus to Alex, the door was opened for Alex's life to be changed.

Lord, give us meekness to interact wisely and share you with others.

- How can you diffuse situations with friends by being meek?
- Where does the spirit of meekness come from?

Annotations

Meekness and modesty are often thought to be negative attributes, when in reality they are hidden strengths that honor God.

Justice and Righteousness

Week 34

Stand Strong

For the LORD is righteous,
he loves justice;
the upright will see his face.

PSALM 11:7

*C*urtis pulled a bag from his pocket and held it out to Robert. "Here, man, try some. It's no big deal."

Robert had never seen drugs before, but he immediately recognized what it was. For a second he was tempted, but then he remembered the night he'd prayed and asked God to keep him pure and righteous, to keep him from giving in to temptation.

"No thanks, man," Robert answered. "It's just not my thing. I respect my brain too much for that."

One of the greatest challenges for all of us is how to keep justice and righteousness in our lives at home and when we're with friends.

The short answer is simple—by doing the right thing and standing up for what is right. However, sometimes when we're with a crowd of friends who seem to ignore what is right in order to do what they think is fun or feels good, it gets really hard.

If you're a godly young person, you want to follow God's plan. You know what is right and wrong, and want to be a good example for others. Decide today what you will and won't do. Making those decisions long before you're put on the spot will strengthen you when the time comes to choose righteously.

Decide to follow God's plan, and ask Him to give you strength.

Lord, please help me to stand strong.

- Share a situation when you had to stand strong.
- How can you prepare in advance to choose righteousness?

Tuesday

It's Not Fair

And the heavens proclaim his righteousness,
for he is a God of justice.

PSALM 50:6

"*I*t's just not fair!"

How many times have you said (or maybe screamed) those words to your parents? Unfortunately for some children, unfairness and injustice rank high on their comments about their family dynamics.

In this case, unfairness and injustice are a matter of perspective. While it may seem unfair to children that parents will not give the same privileges to a fourteen-year-old and a sixteen-year-old, or even a six-year-old and an eight-year-old, most parents don't make decisions based on what's fair. Parents make decisions based on what is best for each individual child, and even though it may seem unfair, their decisions are made out of love.

You may even have said those words, "It's not fair!" to God. Sometimes life seems out of balance, and friends appear to have it easy while you struggle through every hardship. The things God allows in your life may not seem fair, but if you look at them as opportunities to rely more on Him, you grow more resilient than those who don't seem to work as hard. Adversity builds strength.

Like your earthly parents, God wants the best for you. You can trust Him on that.

Lord, I want to trust you more. Remove the word unfair from my vocabulary.

- Why do parents sometimes make decisions that seem unfair?
- How can you handle those moments with a righteous spirit?

A Widow's Prayer

A righteous man knows the rights of the poor;
a wicked man does not understand such knowledge.

PROVERBS 29:7 ESV

*I*n Luke 18, Jesus tells the story of the widow's prayer. Time after time, she stood before a judge, asking him to grant her justice. The judge didn't know God and didn't really care about individuals like her. He was not a fair judge.

He continually refused to grant the widow's request, but she persisted. Finally, the judge decided the only way to get the widow to stop bothering him was to grant her a judgment, so she received justice from an ungodly judge.

God used the heathen judge to accomplish His purpose for the widow. She received her due and was satisfied. Her patient and persistent prayers profited her, in the end.

Have you ever been in a situation where you felt hopeless? You prayed, but it seemed like everyone else who was involved didn't even care about the outcome.

There is always hope when you have Jesus. The widow's situation looked bleak, but she persevered, knowing God could take care of her. She may not have thought He would use the unfair judge that did not know Him, but she trusted God and did her part by bringing her need before the judge.

God took care of the widow, and He can take care of you. Trust Him to do that.

Lord, help us to persevere and to trust you.

- Tell about a situation where you felt as if a wrong would never be made right.
- What are three ways you know God can be trusted?

Pray for America

He has shown you, O mortal, what is good.
And what does the Lord require of you?
To act justly and to love mercy and to
walk humbly with your God.

MICAH 6:8

*N*ews reports highlight a lot of unhappy people. It's obvious these people don't trust God to take care of our world. They believe they must get together and voice their opinions and displeasure, even if it means hurting others. To a foreigner watching our news shows, it may appear that we live in an extremely violent land.

What they don't see is that many righteous and just people live in this country. In a poll by ABC News, 83 percent of the people polled identified themselves as Christians.[*] Wouldn't it be wonderful if all 83 percent committed to praying for the righteousness of the leadership in our nation?

If every Christian in this country would pray and ask others to pray, it could have a domino effect or chain reaction. Could you do that? Pray for those in authority over us. Ask God to give them great wisdom each day. Today would be a good time to start. God hears every prayer, and He wants to bless this country.

Lord, we know you are grieved by what goes on in America and the world. Help our leaders be righteous and just.

- Name two friends you could ask to pray for our country.
- Why do you think our country is experiencing so much unrest?

---

[*] Gary Langer, "Poll: Most Americans Say They're Christian," *ABC News*, http://abcnews.go.com/US/story?id=90356.

God Has a Plan

Yet the LORD longs to be gracious to you; therefore he will
rise up to show you compassion. For the LORD is a God
of justice. Blessed are all who wait for him!

ISAIAH 30:18

*A*braham was a righteous man. Many times in the Bible, God
told Abraham to do something unusual, but his faithfulness
to God always brought him through. He understood God's desire
was for him and his family to live justly wherever He led them.

Jillian's family was a modern-day-Abraham family. She
remembers the first time they moved. "It'll be great for all of us,"
Jillian's dad had said. "There's nothing more exciting than following God's direction for your life."

It didn't seem so exciting to nine-year-old Jillian, who had to
leave friends and move halfway across the country. Where was
the justice in that?

Even so, if you ask grown-up Jillian about it, she says, "Looking
back, it seemed like a bad thing. But every time, my dad assured
me we were following God's plan for our family. And each time
we moved, I made wonderful new friends. I learned that God
knows best for me, and I learned to adapt. Following God's plan
is always the best way."

Lord, help us trust in your righteousness and justice.

- Have you ever not wanted to do something but, looking
  back, you've realized it was part of God's plan?
- How can your family be more in tune to God's plan for
  you?

Annotations

Righteousness and *justice* are biblical words that aren't heard much today, but they're good goals for believers. Others need to see these qualities lived out by God's people.

Service

and

Selflessness

Week
35

Monday

Service

Let each of you look out not only for his own interests,
but also for the interests of others.

PHILIPPIANS 2:4 NKJV

$\mathcal{M}$emorial Day is observed on the last Monday of May to remember the men and women in our armed forces who gave their lives for our country. For Nathan, the day is personal.

Nathan's uncle Sam was in the military. Sam completed one tour overseas and then signed up for another. Nathan remembered the day his mom tried to talk Sam out of the second enlistment. She had worried about him during his first tour and had been relieved when he came home safely. Nathan would always remember what his uncle said that day. "I've seen the horrendous impact of war. I have to go back, Sis, so you and my nephew will be safe. It's my privilege and duty to serve my country."

Nathan had cried the day his uncle hugged the family goodbye. He worried about the danger Sam would face as a pilot in a war zone. He'd cried even harder when he heard his uncle's plane had been shot down over enemy territory. He'd never forget the intense emotions he felt at the airport when he saw Sam's flag-draped coffin roll across the tarmac.

In a manner reminiscent of the sacrifice that Jesus made, his uncle had given his life so others could be free. Jesus said in John 15:13, "Greater love has no one than this, than to lay down one's life for his friends" (NKJV).

Lord, thank you for those who serve.

- Why did Sam enlist a second time?
- Why was the sacrifice worth it?

With Honor

This is how we know what love is: Jesus Christ laid
down his life for us. And we ought to lay down
our lives for our brothers and sisters.

1 JOHN 3:16

Nathan's uncle served our country with honor. That required putting others before himself. Sam was willing to give his life if necessary. He realized that some things are worth fighting and dying for, things like our faith, our freedoms, and our families.

That selflessness cost him many things. He gave up time with his family and others he loved. He went on missions where fear must have filled him as he flew over enemy territory. Sam left the comfort of home and went into a primitive area where the temperatures soared to 108 degrees and the enemy was relentless.

He realized that freedom isn't free; it's sometimes paid for at great price.

Consider what would have happened if he (and thousands of other men and women) hadn't served with selflessness? We wouldn't have the necessary defenders if our country was attacked. Evil would run rampant in the world. Our freedom and liberty would be at stake, and civilization as we know it would be as well.

Aren't you grateful that Jesus and the brave men and women in our armed forces considered that we were worth dying for—and that they gave their lives for us? Let's never take that for granted.

Father, keep me aware that freedom isn't free.

- What did being selfless cost Sam?
- Why does freedom come at great cost?

Into the Fire

"If we are thrown into the blazing furnace,
the God we serve is able to deliver us from it."

DANIEL 3:17

*K*ing Nebuchadnezzar designed a ninety-foot-tall gold statue and erected it in Babylon. He had a herald shout to all the people that as soon as they heard the sound of a horn, flute, or other instruments, they were to bow and worship the king's golden image. Anyone who didn't do so would be thrown into a blazing furnace.

The people did as Nebuchadnezzar commanded—all but three men named Shadrach, Meshach, and Abednego. These men only worshipped the true God, and they refused to bow down before the king's gods. They were willing to give their lives, but they also knew that the God they served was able to deliver them.

Nebuchadnezzar was furious and ordered that they be thrown into the fiery furnace. It was so hot that the men who threw them in perished, but Shadrach, Meshach, and Abednego were not harmed by the flames and didn't even smell like smoke.

They weren't alone in that furnace. The king was stunned when he saw a fourth person walking with them in the flames. God had joined them there—and we can count on Him to be with us, no matter what circumstances we face.

Lord, give me courage to serve you.

- Why were these men willing to face the fiery furnace?
- Who did they encounter there, and why is that important for us?

A Willing Heart

Present your bodies a living sacrifice, holy,
acceptable to God, which is your reasonable service.

ROMANS 12:1 NKJV

Sam's life of service began with a deep love for his nation and his family. He knew the risks before he signed up for a second enlistment, but with a selfless spirit, he said, "I will go." He gave his life for what he loved more.

Shadrach, Meshach, and Abednego could have bowed down and worshipped the golden image like everyone else. It would have been the easy way out. Instead they chose to do the right thing, to live for God even when it was difficult, even when it meant they might have to give their lives for what they believed.

That's a scenario for all of us to think about. How would we respond if God asked us to serve Him by doing something selfless or possibly dangerous?

There's one thing we need to remember though. We don't go through those frightening moments alone. We can know without any doubt that God is with us every step of the way.

Today would be a good time to thank Him for those who left us an example of selflessness, and it would be the perfect opportunity to thank the families of those who gave their lives so we could be free.

Lord, help me to serve you willingly.

- What did Sam, Shadrach, Meshach, and Abednego have in common?
- What can we learn from them?

A Life of Service

Whatever you do, work at it with all your heart,
as working for the Lord, not for human masters, since you
know that you will receive an inheritance from the Lord
as a reward. It is the Lord Christ you are serving.

COLOSSIANS 3:23–24

Sam and the men in the fiery furnace served with honor, and now it's time for *us* to serve God and our country. How can we accomplish that?

We can volunteer at church, give our dollars, go on mission trips, and help those who need a hand. We can serve our country by becoming aware of what is going on in our society and educating ourselves in civics and history. Our Christian values are under attack, and one doesn't have to watch the news for long to see that we as a nation need to turn back to God.

It's important to be involved. Volunteer for your local political party (be sure to study their stated values first). Join a civic club and give back to your community. Pray for those who lead our nation. Pray for the brave men and women who protect our country. Do something nice for a military family. Buy a meal for them. Go fishing with their children. Mow their lawn. Let them know you appreciate their sacrifice.

How could *you* serve with a selfless heart?

Lord, open my eyes to ways I can serve you.

- Why is it important for us to serve God and our country?
- What are other ways you can serve?

Annotations

Serve God faithfully, and then when He calls on you to do something selfless, be willing to obey Him without question.

Wisdom and Insight

Week 36

Eureka!

If any of you lacks wisdom, let him ask of God.

JAMES 1:5 NKJV

*A*rchimedes was just stepping into his bath when the new notion hit him like a wrecking ball. He jumped out, so excited with the practicality of his groundbreaking discovery that he ran into the streets of Syracuse, still naked, shouting, "Eureka! Eureka!"

Eureka means "I have found it!" Archimedes suddenly recognized that the displacement of the water level of his bath corresponded exactly with the volume of the body part he inserted into the bath. In other words, he was suddenly able to calculate the exact volume of objects, despite their unusual shapes. Imagine that in those times, while they boasted relative precision when measuring weight, no such accuracy existed for measuring volume, which meant that density was also a relative unknown. Density was very useful in determining the value of precious metals.

This discovery of something right under our noses is known as an insight. It is like *seeing inside* of something or some situation. This kind of empowering and innovative insight can happen anytime, and it is a blessing by God. You may feel a kind of flush in realizing some new understanding, but you should always remember to get dressed before running outside to tell everyone!

Father, give me new insights every day.

- Why do we sometimes ignore God's wisdom?
- Why is God's Word such a valuable resource?

Tuesday

Figuring It Out

Set your mind on things above, not on things on the earth.

COLOSSIANS 3:2 NKJV

*C*indy glanced at her watch, again, with a final resignation. Just then, Casey came happily strolling around the corner. "Hey, Cinds. Sorry I'm late."

"Yeah. Me too," Cindy began, tentatively. She and Casey had only been dating a little while and were just getting to know each other, but tonight God had given her insight.

Casey shrugged and smiled, charmingly. "So, you ready to go?"

"Well, we've missed the movie now." Cindy was speaking slowly, steeling herself.

"That's no big deal," Casey casually confirmed. "I didn't really want to see your *chick flick*, anyway.

Cindy stood up, relying on God's strength and her new insight. "Casey, here's the thing. I like punctuality, and I really wanted to see that movie. Plus, I can't stay out late tonight, as you know, because of my job at church tomorrow morning. You just don't seem to care about any of those things. So"—she took a breath—"you aren't the guy for me."

"What?" Casey couldn't comprehend how he, the star quarterback, was getting dumped.

"I'm sorry," Cindy continued. "I like my *image* of who you *should* be, but in reality, we are not compatible, and it's just not worth it. I thank God I realized that sooner rather than later."

Father, give me the insight to make wise decisions.

- What happens when we're distracted by the image of what we want?
- When has a sudden insight changed your path?

The Dilemma

Happy is the man who finds wisdom.

PROVERBS 3:13 NKJV

In 1 Kings chapter 3, King Solomon faced quite a dilemma when he judged a case between two women. They shared a house, and both had been pregnant. Their babies were born three days apart. During the night, one of the women rolled over on top of her baby and it died. When she realized what happened, before the other mother woke, she swapped the infants, taking the live one to her chest and leaving her dead baby in the other woman's bed. In the morning, the second mother discovered the dead baby in her bed, but she immediately knew he wasn't hers.

Both women claimed to be the mother of the living infant, so they went before King Solomon for adjudication. They argued back and forth.

The first mother yelled, "This is my child! Your baby is dead!"

The other woman denied that vehemently.

Solomon asked that a sword be brought to him. He stated plainly, "Both of you claim that this is your child." Then he ordered, "Cut the living child in two, and give half to one and half to the other."

One mother screamed, "Please, my lord, give her the living baby! Don't kill him!"

The other one said, "Cut him in two."

Solomon replied, "Give the living baby to the first woman. Do not kill him; she is his mother." That was wisdom that only God could have given him.

God, give me wisdom like Solomon.

- How did Solomon know what to do?
- Why did he have such awesome insight?

253

Asking for Wisdom

"Therefore give to Your servant an understanding heart
to judge Your people, that I may discern
between good and evil."

1 KINGS 3:9 NKJV

Solomon was a man of great wisdom, but it's important for us to understand his heart in that regard. In the third chapter of 1 Kings, one of the first things we learn about Solomon is that he loved God and did his best to walk after Him. That's the perfect starting point for all of us.

God came to Solomon in a dream one night and told him to ask for anything he wanted. Many of us would have made an instant request for a million dollars, but that's not what Solomon did. He started by praising God for how he had blessed him and his father, David, and then he shared how he often felt like a little child as he ruled over the children of Israel. He asked God for wisdom and discernment so he would know good from evil.

That pleased God's heart so much that He granted great wisdom and two more things to Solomon. Solomon became known as the wisest throughout the land, but the Bible tells us God favored Solomon also with wealth and honor—two things he hadn't asked for that night.

Have you ever *asked* God for wisdom? Today would be the perfect time to do that.

Father, give me discernment to know right from wrong.

- Why did Solomon's request please God?
- Why did God also give Solomon wealth and honor?

Sharing God's Wisdom

A wise son heeds his father's instruction.

PROVERBS 13:1 NKJV

There are consequences when we don't act with wisdom, but when we choose wisdom each day, we can touch lives and bring glory to God. God gave Cindy insight and wisdom to make a difficult, necessary decision, that saved a lot of heartache in the long run. Solomon had the intelligence and sagacity to devise a simple plan to discern the liar between the two new mothers.

How can we obtain insight and wisdom? As Solomon showed, God is the source of that, and the quest begins with *asking* Him to give us wisdom. He's provided the handbook in His Word for all that we need. We need to study the treasures there and share them with others.

A wise person will think before taking action—and those who are most wise will never take action until God has given them the insight to know what to do.

Other ways to seek wisdom include praying with friends and family, and seeking counsel from godly teachers, pastors, parents, and grandparents. Many of them have learned from their mistakes, and they can help you avoid those same pitfalls.

As we conclude this devotional book, look back and see how God has already used the topics on these pages to provide insight and wisdom for you. Now take what you've learned and put it to use. Touch others and your world as you venture forth and teach others from love.

Father, give me a wisdom that will impact my world for you.

- Why should you seek insight and wisdom?
- How can you use that to touch the lives of others?

Annotations

Insight helps us to realize that we need wisdom in a situation. Wisdom gives us the follow-through to act in a way that pleases God.

Acknowledgments

For their fine work, I acknowledge the efforts of Michelle Cox, Carol Hatcher, Linda Gilden, and David Sluka. I also would like to acknowledge all the homeschooling families that encourage and uplift each other, Classical Conversations, and the Bortins family, for being inspirational in my homeschooling journey. I pray for all our inspired school teachers and all our nation's students that they may use their educational opportunities to know God better and draw closer to Him.

About the Author

Sam (Jenkins) Sorbo studied biomedical engineering at Duke University before pursuing a career in modeling, which afforded her the opportunity to travel and learn languages; she is fluent in five. Eventually, she moved to Los Angeles for acting, and earned roles in numerous films and TV shows, including *Bonfire of the Vanities*, *Twenty Bucks*, *Chicago Hope*, and *Hercules: The Legendary Journeys*.

As guest star on *Hercules*, she met Kevin Sorbo, who swept her off her feet. They married in 1998, and she moved to New Zealand. While living in Auckland, Sam published a humorous and educational photo book, *Gizmoe: The Legendary Journeys, Auckland*.

The family grew to include three children. In 2016 Sam authored *They're YOUR Kids: An Inspirational Journey from Self-Doubter to Home School Advocate*. The Sorbos home educate.

She hosted *The Sam Sorbo Show*, a weekday nationally syndicated radio program. Most recently, Sam cowrote, produced, and costarred in (with Kevin) *Let There Be Light*, due out Christmas 2017. The film features Dionne Warwick, Travis Tritt, and the two Sorbo boys, is directed by Kevin Sorbo, and is exec-produced by Sean Hannity (LetThereBeLightTheMovie.com).